GREAT RACING DRIVERS

GREAT
RACING
DRIVERS

edited by DAVID HODGES

 TEMPLE PRESS BOOKS · LONDON 1966

Published for
TEMPLE PRESS BOOKS
by
George Newnes Ltd.
Tower House, Southampton Street, London, W.C.2
© 1966, George Newnes Ltd.

Printed in Great Britain by Cox & Wyman Limited
London, Fakenham and Reading

CONTENTS

*Notes on the contributors appear on
pages 175–176*

INTRODUCTION

T H E intention of this book is quite simply to present objective profiles of leading drivers of every era of motor racing. Thus it is not entitled 'The Greatest Racing Drivers', although twenty of those included might well be the top twenty of any list of the greatest drivers of the past—certainly the stature of none of them can be denied. Drivers whose careers had not ended when it went to press have deliberately been excluded.

One of the criteria by which a driver may be judged 'great' is success in classic races. Apart from this, hard facts are not a sound guide and must be abandoned for cumulating generalizations, any of which must occasionally be open to specific refutation. Style or technique is a quality which can hardly be measured; adaptability, to new cars or circuits as well as to conditions, is one which to a certain extent can be gauged 'by the record' but is as well assessed through impressions. Recently it has so often become apparent during practice when some drivers pound away in healthy and competitive cars yet scarcely improve between first and last practice, while the outstanding men may start slowly but on race day are on the front of the grid. The great drivers have not normally accepted that those ahead of them cannot be caught and most certainly have not habitually settled for good places: rather they have fought against odds to improve their positions and have often compensated for mechanical deficiencies or defaults. Then again, motor sport is like any other in that the names and deeds of its great men become part of its lore . . .

Once in a racing car, these drivers were 'professionals', however admirably 'amateur' (in a fading sense) some of them may have been at other times, however carefree their first ventures in motor sport may have been. As far as their machines—and in some cases temperament—allowed they were capable of achieving the consistency which is now virtually prerequisite to success. Nowadays one can get an inkling of what this entailed in, say, the thirties, by watching the behaviour—the antics even—of the cars of that period in historic car races on modern smooth circuits. It was in cars very similar to these that the modern refined and sophisticated style of driving was developed, perhaps most elegantly and successfully by Louis Chiron. Again, on some counts it can be argued that the first of the 'modern' drivers raced even earlier and that Felice Nazzaro and David Bruce-Brown in particular were ahead of their time in their approach to racing as well as in their driving.

While each chapter can be considered complete in itself, many are in fact subject to qualification by comment in another—where contributors have apparently disagreed . . . so be it. Most of the profiles were contributed by writers with special knowledge of their subjects, some through experience of racing with or against them.

Lists of successes are given at the end of most chapters (shared drives, e.g. at Le Mans, are not specified) but not for the one track specialist, who, incidentally, is included in his own right as well as a representative of the 'other half', or for the early drivers: before the First World War there were so few races in each year that all are inevitably mentioned in the discussions of drivers' careers. These are not intended as hard and fast yardsticks with which to compare one driver with another, for as such they would be quite untenable unless simultaneous abstruse mental acrobatics could provide a common denominator by which the very different conditions of each decade could be equated. The sport has changed so much in sixty years that no attempt to place its stars in order of merit could convince; the game of selecting 'first and second teams', fascinating though it can be in discussion, has not been played here. Thus this selection will not please everybody—this would indeed be difficult in any sphere in which personalities feature conspicuously . . .

Motor sport can at times be appallingly tragic—fortunately but rarely although some would have us believe the lurid contrary. Of the drivers recalled in this book, who raced much more than most of their contemporaries, nine died at the wheels of racing cars, five in races. Motor sport can thus be utterly demanding; normally it can be far more exacting than almost any other activity—for the men at the top today this can be as true as it ever has been in the past, albeit in different ways. All of the men who reached the top at any time were dedicated, all had a competitive spirit and ability—compounded of instinct, judgement, anticipation, precision, physical and mental co-ordination and sheer old-fashioned bravery—to a degree which lifted them above their countless fellow drivers. All were great drivers.

D. W. H.

GREAT RACING DRIVERS

The Red Devil

CAMILLE JENATZY

by JACQUES ICKX

SOME take him for a German racing driver and pronounce his name in the German way, as 'Iena'. They are mistaken. Camille Jenatsky was Belgian (his family was of Hungarian origin and had been established in Brussels since the time of Marie-Thérèse), and his name is pronounced in the French way.

He was born on November 4, 1868 of a father who had founded the first rubber factory installed in Belgium and who was, by vocation, a lover of horses. Having, for his part, grown up with the velocipede (boneshaker) Camille, on the other hand, participated in the bicycle craze, took up racing, and won races. One fine day he was seen to leave his bicycle in the middle of a race in order to plunge into the canal which bordered on the course and save the life of an unfortunate person who was drowning there.

But Camille Jenatzy was, at the same time, of a studious nature and when he obtained his degree as a civil engineer he abandoned sports (for ever as he thought) in order to take life seriously. However, his duties in the family business not fulfilling his personal ambitions, he went to Paris in 1897 in order to take part in the 'gold rush' which the advent of the motor car started.

But, instead of setting forth, as did other pioneers of the period, on the conquest of the road, of distance, and of speed, his positive nature turned towards the more immediate interests. Leaving aside the adventure and the glory, it was to the manufacture of electric carriages that he devoted the activities of his General Transport Company. At the time of the first city-to-city races any thought of motor sport was far from his mind, when a combination of circumstances led him very suddenly back to his first love, sport, this time with cars.

On November 28, 1898, in fact, the journal *France Automobile* organized an absolutely unprecedented competition: a hill-climb up 1,800 metres of the Chanteloup hill. This short distance signified that an electric vehicle was not barred *a priori* from taking part, and Camille Jenatzy realized that this was an opportunity to exploit the type's exclusive characteristic of being able to develop considerable power for a short period.

He did not let this opportunity escape him and he carried off the event quite conclusively, averaging over 16 m.p.h. and leaving behind him one of those twin-engined Léon Bollée tri-cars which in speed normally eclipsed other cars of the period.

Encouraged by this first success, *France Automobile* organized a second speed contest. This was a matter of verifying if the progress of the motor had brought mechanical traction up to the level of the cyclist and if the nascent motor car was capable of beating the 66-second kilometre record which had been set up by the world record-holder, Albert Champion. The motor car, however, could not run on the Parc des Princes track and it was therefore necessary to find a straight flat track in the neighbourhood of Paris. The central avenue, narrow but well-kept, of the Parc Agricole d' Achères was placed at the organizer's disposal.

The distance gave rise to a new idea: to run the event over a distance of 2 kilometres, from a standing start with two time checks, the first midway and the second at the end, so that the times could be established for the first, standing-start, kilometre and for the second with a flying start. The record-holding cyclist was comfortably beaten by 9 seconds by the Jeantaud electric car belonging to the Marquis of Chasseloup-Laubat; Jenatzy fell out for some reason which we have not been able to discover. However, the next day he issued a challenge to the winner (the usual thing between gentlemen of the period); Chasseloup accepted. For *France Automobile* this was a heaven-sent opportunity; a regulation designed to prolong the match by authorizing the loser to issue a fresh challenge within a period of thirty days, and obliging the winner to accept it, was drawn up on the spot. The matter could thus be extended for as long as one or the other of the contestants pleased.

I will not repeat the details of these successive encounters in which each of them in turn got the best of it, and which led Jenatzy to build the very first specialized record-breaking motor car. This was simply a shell packed with accumulators and mounted on four small wheels in such a manner as to make possible the direct action of a motor mounted on the shaft. These four small wheels, furthermore, were fitted with tyres expressly manufactured by Michelin. This *avant-garde* creation was christened Jamais Contente ('The Never Content')

Waiting to start in the 1903 Gordon Bennett . . .

—an aside aimed by Camille Jenatzy at his wife, who was not of an easy nature.

After several false starts 'Jamais Contente' covered the kilometre in 34 seconds on April 29, 1899, astonishing the spectators to the extent that they did not immediately realize that a speed of 100 kilometres per hour had been exceeded. On May 14 Chasseloup-Laubat informed the organizing journal that he intended to withdraw, thus putting an end to the contest. But Jenatzy, in the meantime, had become the man of the day. Is it surprising that he found himself again consumed by his passion for sport and that whilst continuing to make his cars and de-livery vehicles, he bought a 16-h.p. Mors in order to take part in the city-to-city races?

But success eluded him. He finished last in the Tour de France (not without his persistence in continuing in spite of all kinds of damage being noted); he was classified as seventh in the Paris–San Malo race, then fifth in the Paris–Ostend race. The following year he took part, very discreetly and almost informally, in the first Gordon-Bennett Cup. This attempt was a fiasco. After which, Jenatzy disappeared from the sporting scene.

He returned to Brussels, and, behind the scenes, prepared his own petrol-driven car.

It would appear that the prototype of this car was built by the Fabrique Nationale d'Armes de Guerre, better known under the name of F.N. at Herstal. It made its first appearance, on July 31, 1902, in the Circuit des Ardennes. But in spite of its 60 horsepower (exceeded, however, by the 70 horsepower of the Panhard) it performed only very

. . . and in the 1904 Gordon Bennett

5

modestly from the outset, completing the first lap ninth amongst the seventeen cars which started. At the beginning of the second, the car lost a wheel at full speed and crashed into a pine wood where it was found literally curled up into a ball.

Its driver, however, escaped without injury. A legend at once was born: this Jenatzy was the devil in person, and as he had red hair and a red, pointed beard, the public created the title of the 'Red Devil'.

The misadventure in the Circuit des Ardennes had the secondary effect of dissuading Jenatzy from following his career as a car manufacturer—had he discovered that his car was faulty? Instead he took up the manufacture of tyres in the family business. As to his sporting career, it continued with Mercedes, who placed at his disposal one of the twelve cars prepared for the Paris–Madrid race.

Then came the fourth Gordon Bennett Cup contested on July 21, 1903 over a circuit in Ireland. The strange regulations of this Challenge which had the national automobile clubs as contestants will be remembered. Each of them could enter three vehicles only, three cars which had to be obligatorily of their own nationality with all their equipment, even to the tyres, while the drivers could be foreigners, eligible from the moment they became members of the club!

But it is also necessary to appreciate that as from then, the qualification for a member of an automobile club was reserved for gentlemen only. Thus, when the Consul Jellinek decided to attack the Gordon Bennett Cup in force he put three 90-h.p. cars at the disposal of the Automobile Club of Germany. The latter straightaway rejected the two professional drivers of the company, Werner and Heironymous, whom it refused to accept as members, and therefore Mercedes and the D.A.C. had finally to let themselves be represented by foreign gentlemen drivers, the Englishman Foxhall-Keene and the two Belgians, de Caters and Jenatzy.

In a fire which ravaged the Bad Canstatt factory some days before the race, the famous specially prepared '90' cars were destroyed. But Jellinek did not allow himself to be upset by this and sent instead '60' touring cars which had been hastily lightened. This apparently risky move proved in the event to be quite safe because from the second lap of the race they virtually had no further opposition. Jenatzy, at the top of his form took the lead and did not lose it, gaining on each lap over the Panhard of René de Knyff (the latter, another Belgian, representing the A.C.F.) who, right to the end, was his closest competitor.

At the end of the penultimate lap there was a moment of hesitation because Jenatzy had no more tyres in reserve, Mercedes having been prevented by the sports officials from using the German Michelin tyres, of which the team had brought a complete stock. But Jenatzy took it upon himself to start off again and to finish the race on his worn set, taking care to use them economically. He was completely successful: the 'Red Devil' knew how to keep a cool head.

Is it necessary to say that once he had won the Gordon Bennett Cup, which in a way gave him the World Championship of his time, Jenatzy was incapable of giving up racing? A winner always believes that 'Lady Luck' will continue to favour him, and is eager to pursue her. This is what happened to Camille Jenatzy. But races were infrequent at the beginning of the century, and the years passed by without his glorious triumph being repeated.

In the 1904 Gordon Bennett over the Taunus circuit, he finished second in a race which was dominated by Théry (Brasier). In the 1905 Gordon Bennett, this time with a '120' car, he retired without having been placed any better than twelfth. Further failures followed in the Circuit des Ardennes and in the Vanderbilt Cup which for the first time brought the best European drivers to the United States. In 1906 the first Grand Prix de l'A.C.F. saw Jenatzy classified 'next to last' on the first day and refusing to start on the second. He was then tenth in the Circuit des Ardennes—a race in which only twelve cars finished. However, a fifth place in the Vanderbilt Cup, behind Wagner, Lancia, Duray, and Clément, brought hope back to his heart.

Mercedes remained as loyal to Jenatzy as Jenatzy was loyal to them, but the good days had passed for both. In the 1907 Kaiserpreis the 'Red Devil' qualified for the final and finished in the fourteenth place; in the Grand Prix de l'A.C.F. he did not finish. He believed in his revival in the Circuit des Ardennes in which he started in dashing style. In the first lap he established a time which was not beaten during the day, but then his engine failed and he retired again.

Then came the 1908 season and with the reorganization of Mercedes, what appeared to be a chance to star again. However, the new board of directors of Untertürkheim had chosen new men and Jenatzy waited on the side-lines. Even so he could not give up racing—Mors having entered for the Grand Prix at the last moment with a team of three hastily prepared cars, he asked if he could drive one of them.

Jenatzy finished the race, but in sixth place, lost in the throng. This was to be his last race, because the Grand Prix was to be abandoned for four years and when it came to life again in 1912 it was too late for a man of 44 years of age to pick up the reins again.

However, final retirement from racing did not spare the 'Red Devil' from a tragic end. On October 7, 1913 he took part in a wild boar hunt organized in the Ardennes by his friend Madoux, Director of the daily paper *l'Etoile Belge*. As night fell Camille Jenatzy left his hiding place without awaiting the signal at the end of the hunt. In the twilight Madoux took him for an animal and shot at him with his rifle. Wounded by a direct hit, the veteran champion was in a desperate condition and survived the accident for only a few minutes.

It does not fail to be moving that he breathed his last in his own Mercedes, where he had been laid. Because he had always remained faithful to the Mercedes car which he had driven to the Olympus of motor racing.

Peak years. In 1907 . . .

FELICE NAZZARO

by   W. F. BRADLEY

WHEN the small firm of Ceirano of Turin was absorbed by the rapidly growing *Fabbrica Italiana Automobile Torine* (F.I.A.T.) in 1899, the fate of two promising young men was involved. They were Vincenzo Lancia and Felice Nazzaro, two youths of about 19 who were employed on all kinds of test and experimental work.

Felice Nazzaro was the son of a Turin coal merchant. At 15 years of age he had been put to work with Ceirano where his position was ill-defined—errand boy, mechanic, cleaner, apprentice—and he was set to learn his trade in the hard way. Tall, quiet, almost aristocratic in manner, the youthful Felice spoke excellent French, as was then common among the Piedmonti, in addition to his native Italian, and quickly won the respect of his employers and fellow workers. He was under the direct control of Lancia, only slightly his elder and, when they joined F.I.A.T., they continued their special experimental work.

Lancia had quickly earned a reputation as a daring, spectacular and successful race driver, winning a race from Vicenzo to Padua in 1900 and thus giving F.I.A.T. its first competition victory. Nazzaro followed his senior and then proved his own worth in 1901. The Duke of the Abruzzi, owner of a Fiat, arranged a private race for a stake of 5000 lire, against a racing Panhard et Levassor belonging to Cavaliere Coltelletti. The race, controlled by the Automobile Club of Italy, was run over the Turin–Bologna road and Senator Agnelli and Lancia rode the Fiat as passengers.

Unknown to the principals, Felice Nazzaro made an application to be officially timed over the same route, with a new 12-h.p. Fiat. When travelling at about 50 m.p.h. over greasy roads and in heavy rain, the Duke's Fiat hit the kerb and was brought to a standstill with a bent axle. The 'race' did not end in victory for the Panhard, however, for Nazzaro's Fiat averaged 33 m.p.h. and was four minutes faster than the French car.

During this period when racing cars were impressive by their size and their drivers had to be endowed with physical strength and recklessness, Felice Nazzaro introduced what might be termed the 'gentlemanly' type of driving. He knew how to change gears silently and just as quickly as his noisy rivals and he had an inborn sympathy for the machinery in his hands. As a consequence he very rarely walked back to the pits yet there was nothing timid in his method of driving: it was refined, flexible, fast, without appearing sensational.

When Nazzaro won the Targa Florio, in 1907, clipping 25 minutes off the previous year's time, he had been on the road 8 hours 17 minutes. Practically all the work of changing tyres, taking on supplies of petrol, oil and water had been done by himself and his mechanic. Yet when he removed his cap his black hair was unruffled, his hands were clean and his general appearance was much smarter than that of many who had never strayed beyond the grandstands.

. . . and after the 1922 French Grand Prix

Another feature of Nazzaro's approach to racing was the minute care with which he prepared his car. He was not allowed to make any radical changes, but there was not a nut or a bolt, a cotter pin or a clip that did not receive the closest inspection. Everything was polished and where he could drill without danger, weight was removed.

In the early days of the century races were few and far between, for they were costly to organize and there were practically no gate receipts (and, similarly, no prizes). In 1900 Nazzaro raced but once, from Vicenzo to Padua, finishing second in his class. The following year there was only one race over the 50 miles from Piombino to Grosseto, where Nazzaro finished first in his class.

The last of the series of races for the Gordon Bennett Cup was held in mountainous Auvergne, the Fiat team cars being driven by Lancia, Nazzaro and Cagno. A Fiat win seemed certain when Lancia secured a lead of 13 minutes but he was forced out with a wrecked engine (probably the result of his punishing type of driving) and Théry's Brasier again won while Nazzaro finished second with his companion Cagno 4 minutes behind him.

The first French Grand Prix, a two-day event, was held in 1906 on a circuit near Le Mans, Szisz leading for Renault at the end of the first day and maintaining this position at the end of the race, with Nazzaro second on Fiat and his team-mate Lancia in fifth position. Then, for the second successive year, he was flagged off, sixth, in the Vanderbilt Cup race.

It was in 1907, however, that Nazzaro attained the height of his fame. He began by winning the Targa Florio against formidable competition, for the forty-seven competitors comprised the best drivers of the period, and he beat Lancia by 14 minutes. Then came the Kaiser Cup Race, on the Taunus circuit, wherein Nazzaro was first at an average speed of 52·6 m.p.h. Three weeks later he was on the Dieppe circuit for the French Grand Prix, which he won with his 130-h.p. Fiat at an average of 68·6 m.p.h. Never before had one man won three great races in a single year.

The following year S. F. Edge challenged the whole world to meet his six-cylinder Napier in a speed contest on Brooklands track. The challenge was taken up by Fiat, who decided to build a special car, the SB4, having a four-cylinder engine of 190 by 160 mm. bore and stroke. It was immediately dubbed 'Mephistopheles' while its Napier rival, driven by Frank Newton, was known as 'Samson'. Felice Nazzaro was selected to drive the Italian car. The match aroused tremendous interest, for these were the two fastest cars which had ever appeared on Brooklands track.

Newton, the crack track driver of the Napier Company, took full advantage of the start, shot over the line and got a good lead over the Italian car; on the second lap he extended his lead to about 300 yards. Then Nazzaro opened out, rapidly overhauled the Napier and passed it amid frantic excitement. As he went by the Napier, the official timers declared a speed of 111 m.p.h. and a little later the timers were swearing to 120 m.p.h. When two-thirds of the total distance of 27½ miles had been covered, Newton was well in the rear and then he suddenly pulled off the track with a broken crankshaft. The Italian was officially credited with a speed of 121·64 m.p.h. for a full lap of the Brooklands track.

Nazzaro immediately became the idol of British motorists. He had no

Different eras. 1907 Kaiserpreis

. . . 1907 Targa Florio

. . . and 1922 French Grand Prix

previous experience of track racing (and because he was not familiar with Brooklands was obliged to carry a mechanic), but he was coolness personified, thrilled the spectators who admired the consummate cleverness and nerve with which the Italian steered his car in perilous proximity to the edge of the course. The result was recognized as a blow to British prestige.

In the French Grand Prix which was again run at Dieppe, the two Fiat entries suffered from crankshaft failure, after Nazzaro had been in the lead and Wagner had held fourth position. Later in the season, however, Nazzaro won the Coppa Florio, on the Bologna circuit, with an average of 73·2 miles per hour.

In the Spring of 1911 Nazzaro resigned his position with Fiat to establish his own company. In this respect he was following the example of Lancia who, a few years earlier, had left Fiat to found the Lancia Motor Company and from the beginning had met with immense success. As was to be expected, Nazzaro maintained an interest in racing and in 1913 he won the Targa Florio for the second time, the race on this occasion being a two-day event right round the island of Sicily, a distance of just under 600 miles, where he averaged 31·04 m.p.h. The following year he again started in the Targa, which was run under the same conditions, but failed to finish.

Apparently, however, Nazzaro the manufacturer was not as brilliant as Nazzaro the race driver—his three-car team of three o.h.c., 16-valve cars retired from the 1914 French G.P., although Nazzaro himself did win the 1920 Aosta-Grand St. Bernard hill-climb with one of these cars. When, in 1922, Senator Agnelli invited him to return to Fiat, he therefore accepted and became head of the racing section. The Fiat team which was entered for the 1922 French Grand Prix at Strasbourg thus included Nazzaro, who was then 42 years of age.

He had done practically no racing for several years; car design had completely changed, for instead of engines of up to 16 litres the Grand Prix capacity limit had been reduced to 2 litres. Critics declared that it was foolish for an 'old man' to compete against such youngsters as Bordino, Segrave, Masetti and Chassagne. However, Nazzaro made no comment; a few minutes after the massed start he was leading the pack on the long, fast leg after Enzheim corner. It was a thrilling, cruel race in which the Fiats showed a marked superiority over all others. Of the eighteen starters only three covered the full distance of 500 miles and four complete teams were wiped out—Sunbeam, Rolland-Pilain, Ballot and Aston Martin. From beginning to end a Fiat always had the lead. First it was the veteran Felice Nazzaro; then, according to plan, Bordino set the pace and broke lap record after lap record; Biagio Nazzaro, a newcomer held himself in reserve.

Felice Nazzaro won the race at an average speed of 79·2 m.p.h. It was while he was being shouldered in triumph past the grandstands that news came through of an accident to his nephew Biagio. While running at maximum speed, the rear axle of his car failed, it lost a wheel and crashed. The driver was killed outright. A similar accident happened to Bordino on his last lap, but as he was taking a bend at minimum speed there was no injury to the crew.

In September of the same year, driving the same car, Nazzaro finished second to Bordino in the Italian Grand Prix at Monza, averaging 86 m.p.h. Exactly a year later, in the European Grand Prix on the same circuit Nazzaro again finished second, less than a minute behind

During his break from Fiat (Itala, 1913 French G.P.)

the winner Salamano and at the tremendous average of just over 90 m.p.h. He had led into the last lap, only to be robbed of a last great victory by a broken oil pipe. . . . He appeared again in the 1924 French Grand Prix, but retired after 22 laps (of 35) when running 12th.

Engineer after engineer had been enticed away from Fiat; it was felt that racing did not have the technical or commercial advantages of the early days, with the result that the firm closed its racing department. Felice Nazzaro continued as head of road experimental work until within a few weeks of his death in Turin on March 21, 1940.

The principal racing successes of **FELICE NAZZARO**

1906	2nd:	French G.P.	1914	1st:	Coppa Florio.
1907	1st:	French G.P.; Kaiserpreis; Targa Florio.	1922	1st:	French G.P.
1908	1st:	Targa Bologna.		2nd:	Italian G.P.
	3rd:	Savannah Grand Prize.			
1913	1st:	Targa Florio.	1923	2nd:	Italian G.P.

CHRISTIAN LAUTENSCHLAGER

by RICHARD VON FRANKENBERG

ONE knows of Christian Lautenschlager that he won the French Grands Prix of 1908 and 1914, but very little else.

He was born on April 13, 1877, in the small village of Magstadt, some 14 miles from Stuttgart; and since his parents were poor, was sent there at the age of 14 to learn the trade of locksmith. After an apprenticeship of three and a half years he travelled as a journeyman, as was customary at that time. This was a useful custom, for the young artisans came to learn something of the world and those with sufficient initiative frequently emigrated for some months or years to continue their apprenticeship abroad. In this way, the young Christian Lautenschlager left first of all for Switzerland, working in Zurich and Lucerne, and he then travelled to Chemnitz in Saxonia, where he worked in a bicycle factory. Not until he was 22 did he return to Stuttgart, there to apply for the job of mechanic at the works of Gottlieb Daimler, which at that time was beginning to expand greatly.

Old Daimler liked the 22-year-old Lautenschlager and employed him in the vehicle construction department. When Daimler died in the spring of 1900 Wilhelm Maybach continued as principal construction engineer at the Daimler Motor Works and under him Christian Lautenschlager rose eventually to the position of foreman in the driving department, responsible for the inspection and running-in of new cars.

He had his first race in 1906, when the Daimler works entered three cars for the Circuit of the Ardennes race. The works cars were to be driven by the Belgian Jenatzy, the Englishman Burton and the Unterturkheim foreman, Salzer. Lautenschlager rode as co-driver with Salzer. The pair were only ninth at the finish—the French competition had proved altogether too strong—but they had nevertheless still managed to finish just ahead of the famous Jenatzy.

When the Daimler entered a team of three cars for the 1908 Grand Prix de l'A.C.F., Lautenschlager was given one as a driver in his own right, another was driven by Salzer and the third by Willy Pöge, an owner-driver of that period. There existed at that time a certain rivalry between the owner-drivers, those wealthy sportsmen who had brought motor sport into existence in the 'nineties, and the mechanics who had come up the hard way from the shop floor and were generally employed in the works driving and testing departments. When, at the turn of the century, motor racing started to become 'professional' by virtue of large firms entering their cars, a number of mechanics reached the front ranks. Lautenschlager was a perfect example; the 'other side' was represented by men like Camille Jenatzy who achieved his first world record in 1899, won the Gordon Bennett race in 1903 and owned a tyre factory, or Lord Brabazon who drove an Austin in the French Grand Prix of 1908.

The 1908 Grand Prix de l'A.C.F. was run according to the most extraordinary rules (known as the 'Ostend Rules' since they had been

15

arrived at by an international commission at Ostend the previous year). Engines were allowed a maximum of four cylinders, each cylinder with a maximum bore of 155 mm. (there were no restrictions regarding stroke) and apart from this, ready to race, but without fuel and water, the cars were required to weigh at least 1,100 kg.

The course at Dieppe where this race took place on July 7, 1908, was a pure road circuit typical of the period and running through numerous villages. The lap measured some 48 miles and the race distance was ten laps. Races of such length, under the road conditions of that time and with the 'mammoth' vehicles of the period, were an extreme test (the Mercedes Grand Prix car of 1908 had a 13·3-litre (155 × 180 mm.) engine with an output of 140 h.p. at 1,400 r.p.m.). Lautenschlager was of powerful build, a 'bull' and in remarkably good physical condition: a valuable asset at that time!

He won this Grand Prix by almost nine minutes from the Frenchman Hémery in his Benz; Pöge finished fifth, Salzer retired with engine trouble. This victory in the most important race of 1908, and in front of a partisan crowd, made Lautenschlager famous. Yet during the following years nothing was heard of him. Otto Salzer and Willy Pöge in Mercedes entered for many more races and won, but Lautenschlager remained at the works as driving foreman (although in the course of his work he tested and drove all Mercedes racing cars). Not until 1913 was he sent out to race again, to drive in the 'semi-works' Mercedes team entered for the Grand Prix of France (not the classic A.C.F. race) at Le Mans. The team were modestly successful with some of the last chain-driven 'leviathans' to be seen in road racing—Théodore Pilette, the Belgian agent for Mercedes who was behind this particular venture, finished third, Salzer was fourth and Lautenschlager sixth, a good if not great performance.

On July 4, 1914 dawned the greatest day in the life of Christian Lautenschlager. This Grand Prix de l'Automobile Club de France was already overshadowed by political events—the Austrian Archduke Franz Ferdinand had been assassinated the previous day—but nevertheless some 300,000 spectators were drawn to the 23-mile road circuit near Lyon. No other race run before the First World War had been such a Festival of Motor Sport; it ended with Lautenschlager's victory over the *élite* of European drivers, in a sweeping victory for Paul Daimler's 4·5-litre Mercedes. These 115-h.p. cars had at that time brakes on the rear wheels only while the Peugeot, Delage and Fiat entries were equipped with four-wheel brakes.

Apart from Lautenschlager, the Mercedes team included Otto Salzer, the Frenchman Louis Wagner, Théodore Pilette and Max Sailer, trials engineer at the works since 1910 and the same Sailer who in the 'thirties was to become technical director. Otto Sailer easily led for the first five laps, but was then forced to retire with defective connecting rod: he had obviously overstrained the engine. Now the hero of the crowd, Boillot in the Peugeot, took the lead and after sixteen of the twenty laps held a two-minute lead over Lautenschlager, but then Boillot slowed perceptibly; on the eighteenth lap Lautenschlager passed him; on the last lap Boillot fell out. Lautenschlager led Wagner and Salzer home to the finish: that then was the famous triple Mercedes victory.

For the Mercedes drivers' return to Stuttgart-Untertürkheim, the entire town hung out its flags in welcome. Lautenschlager was given

Heroic figure. G.P. de l'A.C.F., 1908

honours of a king; all else apart, he won 25,000 gold francs which helped him to build a beautiful house. Yet he remained as thrifty as any other artisan of Swabia.

Even after the First World War Lautenschlager continued to be ranked as the Number One driver at Mercedes. He was sent to the Targa Florio in 1922, where he was placed second in his category but only tenth in the overall classification, while the Italian, Count Masetti won in a Mercedes. In 1923 he travelled to Indianapolis with the Mercedes team, but his car did not finish, while Max Sailer did at least manage eighth place. In the 1924 Targa Florio it was Christian Werner who won with the new supercharged 2-litre Mercedes; Lautenschlager, now already 47 years of age, again finished tenth. He then withdrew from racing, but continued to work for Daimler-Benz until his retirement. He died at the age of 77, in the spring of 1954.

He had led a retiring life, noise and fuss were alien to his nature. This gallant hardened son of Swabia with the huge moustache had been one of the best drivers to be found anywhere before 1914, in which year he had won the race which is still sometimes recalled as 'The Greatest Grand Prix'.

'The Greatest Grand Prix'—
passing the crowded stands at Lyon, August 1914

In the Benz outside his New York City home

DAVID BRUCE-BROWN

by L. SCOTT BAILEY

'THE instant I rested my eyes upon him, an utter stranger, I had a fairly accurate gauge of his character. He was the personification of fine, wholesome and splendid youth and upon him was an unmistakable stamp of good breeding. For he was a fellow of natural poise and courteous deportment, attired nattily yet inconspicuously and spoke in a soft, modulated voice. He introduced himself as David Bruce-Brown, a student at Yale, but he was too much the true gentleman to add that he was the scion of a very wealthy and socially prominent New York family. His code in fact did not tolerate braggadocio of any sort'.

'I was wondering, Mr. Wagner', he said, 'if you would mind telling me when the Fiat team is leaving for Florida'.

Such was the first meeting between Fred J. Wagner, dean of American race starters, and the handsome youth who was to rise to international fame as the runaway schoolboy who became, in the words of Ralph de Palma, 'one of the greatest drivers who ever gripped a steering-wheel'.

After Wagner answered the boy's question, he asked why the information was sought. David Bruce-Brown enthusiastically related his great interest in the sport of racing, but, he confessed, his mother had aspirations for him in fields less dangerous so he had run away from school to make the Florida trip, his boxing instructor at Yale lending him enough money for the fare one way and hotel expenses for the duration of the meeting. He wanted to be a racing driver.

Wagner was impressed with the lad, but wishing to avoid an angry confrontation with an indignant mother, he diplomatically suggested that the boy contact E. R. Hollander, U.S. representative for Fiat.

When the train carrying the racing party for the 1908 Ormond-Daytona trials left Penn Station in New York City, David Bruce-Brown was on board. During the trip the runaway schoolboy completely captivated everyone in whom he confided, and impressed those whom it was important to impress: Emanual Cedrino, Fiat racing driver, Sam Butler, A.A.A. contest board chairman, and Robert Lee Morrell, chairman of the Daytona meeting. Arriving at Daytona, David Bruce-Brown donned old clothes and served a humble and greasy apprenticeship on behalf of F.I.A.T.

Soon telegrams of maternal protest bombarded the Daytona race officials, together with threats of legal action should David Bruce-Brown be permitted behind the wheel of a racing car. But to hold the boy in check was nearly impossible. His enthusiasm was boundless, and his scorn for his mother's lawyers was met with an understanding approval by his associates. Cedrino secretly let him ride as a mechanic in one race; Wagner commented, 'The smile of joy that lighted his face as he leapt into the car was worth a life sentence in any penitentiary.'

At the close of the racing trials, the young enthusiast convinced Hollander that W. K. Vanderbilt, Jr.'s four-year-old amateur record of

Winner of two early 'American Grands Prix'
(Savannah Grand Prize, 1911)

a mile in 39 seconds could easily be broken by Fiat. And the amateur to do it was David Bruce-Brown, of course. As Wagner nodded in assent he wondered 'who were the best lawyers I could engage.'

David Bruce-Brown drove the big Fiat like a seasoned veteran—settling his tall, lanky yet muscular frame confidently behind the wheel and clipping three seconds off Vanderbilt's record. Telegrams of congratulations from a proud mother arrived soon after; there was no mention of lawyers or law suits.

The newspapers heralded David Bruce-Brown's achievement. It was a natural story, the Ivy League schoolboy who preferred the smell of burning oil and tyres to that of a musty library. Good looks, youthful sincerity, abject humility and obvious ability—these all were his. His meteoric climb to fame was perhaps inevitable.

Later, in 1908, he competed in the Shingle hill-climb promoted by the Yale University Automobile Club. Official reports show that D. B. Brown was awarded a gold medal for the fastest time made by an amateur. The following year he entered again with Victor Hémery's old 120-h.p. Benz and won, this time as David Bruce-Brown.

In 1909 he won numerous events in the New England area. And at Ormond-Daytona Beach his 120 Benz was second fastest to Oldfield's Blitzen Benz in the mile trial times. With the same Benz he won the Dewar Trophy in three one-mile heats against de Palma's Fiat and beat de Palma again in the ten-mile Free For All. By the time the International Grand Prize was held in Savannah in 1910, David Bruce-Brown's skill and charm had earned him a place on the Benz team.

He won the race, beating the famous Victor Hémery by one second.

Reporters were having a field day with the David Bruce-Brown story —the saga of the boy wonder striving to overcome the restrictions of wealth. And this enthusiasm abounded at Savannah because of the appearance of Mrs. Bruce-Brown whose sole objective was to convince her son to give up racing. But not even Mrs. Bruce-Brown could be indifferent to the excitement of the race. When she saw her son leading, her feelings reportedly got the better of her. She literally sprinted to the track when he won, embracing him before he could either remove his goggles or get out of the car.

By 1911 Bruce-Brown had joined the Fiat team with Louis Wagner and Caleb Bragg, and again he won the International Grand Prize at Savannah. Again, too, the race was witnessed by a beaming, though apprehensive mother. When asked whether she would allow him to race again, she replied from behind her dust-covered veil, 'I can't say about that now'.

Ralph de Palma found the boy 'a most lovable fellow' with a penchant for 'some of the most original stunts'. Nothing better exemplified this than Bruce-Brown's lopsided bet with de Palma prior to the Savannah race: the winner was to treat the loser to a trip to Europe. The following season David Bruce-Brown made good his wager by taking Mr. and Mrs. de Palma abroad for an extended tour.

It was in that year that Bruce-Brown, in the Fiat team with Wagner and de Palma, entered the fourth G.P. de l'A.C.F., a two-day, 956-mile race over a circuit at Dieppe. The errant schoolboy, as all of racing France knew him by then, led the race from the start. During the first day he averaged 72·4 m.p.h. and set a new circuit record. On the second day, however, he was disqualified for taking on fuel at a non-official stop. Undaunted, he continued on anyway, boyishly believing

So nearly the first American to win the Grand Prix. Before the start at Dieppe, 1912 . . .

. . . and during the race

that the French officials would excuse his unfamiliarity with the re-fuelling rules. They didn't. He was placed third, unofficially.

Later that year David Bruce-Brown prepared to defend the trophy he had twice won in the Milwaukee Grand Prize Cup Road Race.* During one of the practice runs, Wagner, official starter for the race, noticed that Bruce-Brown's tyres were worn through and ordered him back to the garages. But Bruce-Brown pleaded for just one more lap. Racing down the back stretch, Teddy Tetzlaff, a Fiat team-mate, began the chase. The unpredictable, fearless Teddy never gave an inch to anyone, much less a team-mate. Both cars were throwing dust and rocks. Ralph Mulford in his Lozier pulled over to let them pass. Hub to hub, Tetzlaff edged ahead, as the rear right tyre blew on Bruce-Brown's Fiat. The big car lurched into the ditch and in a vain attempt to right it, Bruce-Brown jerked the wheel. The car jumped to the opposite side of the road; both driver and mechanic were thrown out of it, and within hours David Bruce-Brown was dead.

A stunned racing world sang the praises of the youngster who had beaten the best—Wagner, Hémery, de Palma—and who had charmed hundreds more as the son of the blue-blooded society matron who brought to the race track the aura of a gentleman driver.

The David Bruce-Brown story had the romance of a novel. For the historian, however, it now presents a dilemma—the plague of facts recorded and unrecorded.

* A day in *Automobile Quarterly*'s research department is not without interest. In probing the Yale records, we discovered that Caleb S. Bragg, Bruce-Brown's team-mate, was a duly recorded graduate of Yale's class of 1908. When asked for a biography in 1939, Bragg replied, 'Before entering business I spent time travelling in Europe and America. My hobbies are the gasoline sports—automobiling, aviation and power boats'. The class historian delved further: 'Caleb S. Bragg was the first president of Yale's Automobile Club in 1908, set two world's records in a 90-hp Fiat in 1910 and in 1912 won the fourth International Grand Prix at Milwaukee . . .' For example, there are no records at Yale that show David Bruce-Brown as a student. Nor does any boxing team list reveal his name. Even the Shingle Hill event sponsored by the Yale Automobile Club and reported in the school's newspaper makes no mention of his prior association with that institution. The reports state that the club's prize for a Yale Student was awarded to two others during the years David Bruce-Brown won as an outside amateur. The Social Register for the years 1907 to 1913 does list a Mrs. George Bruce Brown and her two children, William Brown and David L. Bruce Brown of 189 East 59th Street, New York City. But David Bruce-Brown's obituary lists his address as Brooklyn. His is a story yet to be fully plumbed.

'. . . *very sure of himself* . . .' (*1913*)

GEORGES BOILLOT

by S. C. H. DAVIS

MANY men have made names for themselves in motor racing, few have been more vivid characters than the great Frenchman, Georges Boillot.

In the years before the First World War there was only one great race in the season, the Grand Prix de l'Automobile Club de France: all others were inferior in status, even though they may have been more arduous. The chances of getting the wheel of a racing car were thus slight and the opportunities to prove driving skill rare indeed. Moreover, in selecting their team drivers, manufacturers naturally favoured men already working for them—intimate knowledge of the cars, as well as mechanical skill, were invaluable so that the riding mechanic was not relied upon completely when trouble struck. This was particularly so in the racing conditions of those days; the principal races were much longer than those we have now, 500 miles being usual, and they often seemed to be run on the hottest day of the year, on circuits of 20 miles or more which became sea beaches of loose stones before the cars had covered half the racing distance.

Georges Boillot was employed by Peugeot, was fully skilled as a mechanic and able to assist in the design of a racing car as well as in its preparation. Strong, square-built, determined, Georges commenced

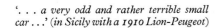

'. . . *a very odd and rather terrible small car* . . .' (*in Sicily with a 1910 Lion-Peugeot*)

his racing career with a very odd and rather terrible small car, the Lion-Peugeot, product of the weirdly intricate regulations governing the Coupe de *l'Auto* races. The single-, or twin-, cylinder engines of these extraordinary cars were so high that in at least one model the driver had to look round the side of the bonnet! They seemed to be kept on the road solely by the strength and skill of their drivers. A move from these devices to the wheel of a real Grand Prix car must, one imagines, have come as a great relief.

Now Boillot was as picturesque a character as you could find anywhere in the wide world. Those who had been brought up on Dumas's *The Three Musketeers* instantly recognized that here was the modern equivalent of that heroic being d'Artagnan with, perhaps, a touch of Cyrano de Bergerac. Very sure of himself—and with reason—Boillot would tackle anything, and the greater the difficulties the more he enjoyed the battle. From the first he seemed at one with his car, his cornering technique was incredibly accurate, his delight in his own prowess obvious to anyone. On the loose stones of a fast corner he could hold the car to an inch, you could see him doing it with every movement vigorous. He seemed to change gear with all his body in action, to delight in showing his mastery of the machine for all to see.

Not surprisingly he had the crowd with him in every race, and this in turn inspired him to even greater efforts. Such a man might seem over boastful, too satisfied with himself, perhaps theatrical. But, odd as it sounds, this all seemed quite natural in Boillot for in him there was no suggestion of boasting but simply an expression of individuality exactly fitting to the man. When he came along to the cafés which most of the racing teams used during the evenings you could tell it was Boillot the moment his car appeared. To the crowds of enthusiasts always present this man seemed to be the very spirit of France.

So it was fitting that he was the first man to prove that the huge monsters normally used in Grands Prix could be beaten by the neater, smaller-engined, cars which were the true ancestors of the machines we know today. The two-day French Grand Prix of 1912 was run on the Dieppe circuit, 478 miles to be covered on the first day and another 478 on the second. Favourites for the race were the giant, scarlet, 15-litre Fiats, against which Peugeot entered 7½-litre cars, the engines of which had four overhead valves per cylinder and an overhead camshaft. And to the great joy of the huge crowd Boillot kept the smaller Peugeot right up on the huge Fiat driven by the American Bruce-Brown all through the first day's racing. Bruce-Brown drove a magnificently regular race, giving away nothing. But always Boillot's dark blue Peugeot was there just behind. It was the kind of race one dreams of, a duel between the two finest drivers of the day. For part of the time I was happily seated close to a fast curve and it was thrilling to note that both cars came round on almost exactly the same line. Lap after lap the Peugeot held the Fiat, obviously being fought round the course by its driver's strength. Next day the duel was repeated until nearly the end when the Peugeot gained each round. With but a few laps to go there was a curious murmur through the crowd, a moment of tenseness, before it was apparent for certain that the Fiat was late. And then enthusiastic cheers as the Peugeot swept by in the lead at last.

Here at last was a French success in a race which had seemed in France's favour from its inception in 1906 but which had too often fallen to foreign cars. Boillot's triumphant return to the team head-

Mont Ventoux, 1912

quarters after the race was unforgettable. From then on he was the acknowledged hero of France, the champion of his country. And he was just the man for the part, bearing himself with that slight air of swagger suitable to the role, yet never overstepping the limit as so many do to whom fame comes suddenly. He was, of course, the leader of the team driving to win with the other two Peugeot drivers in support.

Nineteen thirteen was again his year. Victorious in the Coupe de l'Auto as well as in the French Grand Prix on the Amiens circuit, he made Peugeot supreme and deserved his success. During race week almost every shop seemed to have a photograph of him as chief attraction for their window display, a strong, tough figure with a bristling 'handlebar' moustache and a supreme air of confidence. Somehow or other you could not imagine him being beaten in any international race of importance.

Then came that fatal year 1914.

The Grand Prix was held at Lyon. The entry was magnificent—Peugeot, Mercedes, Vauxhall, Sunbeam, Alda, Schneider, Nagant, Piccard-Pictet, Opel, Nazzaro, Delage—all works teams and most of them good ones.

The 23-mile circuit was one of the finest ever used, a circuit with every kind of curve and corner, a spectacular circuit with one long straight made more interesting by small hills so that it might have been a switchback. To add a thrill the sharp right-hand bend at the end of the straight was called 'le Virage de la Mort'. The staging of the race was magnificent too but there was a strange undercurrent of unease. A few days before the race an unknown and apparently mentally unstable youth had shot an Austrian Archduke. It seemed extraordinary, but the international tension could be felt. As usual the teams welcomed visitors, all that is save Mercedes who held themselves rigidly aloof.

The day of the race dawned brightly. Huge crowds occupied every vantage-point round the circuit. Peugeot's arrival was cheered and clapped to the echo. The Mercedes team were received in silence. Somehow or other it seemed that Boillot, though confident as ever, was not as much at ease during those trying moments when the cars were sorted in pairs for the start. The French champion used gestures more than usual, was intense and serious.

That race will figure always as the most dramatic ever held. The cars were started in pairs until all had gone. Every eye then seemed focused on top of the hill near the grandstands at which the cars would first reappear, and there was a murmur which grew to a roar as Boillot's dark blue car was first round the curve. Thick and fast came the rest of the field. An interval and then a low murmur as the score board showed that not Boillot but Sailer with a Mercedes was leading. Advised of this by his pit signal Boillot eagerly accepted challenge. Round after round the Peugeot gained on its rival. And then what seemed an universal gasp. The Mercedes was missing, Boillot led.

But it was obvious that Mercedes were working to a tactical plan. Right up on the French car's tail came three more Mercedes, white, shark-like, ominous. That Boillot knew the situation was obvious. The man was driving as one inspired, driving with every part of himself, with superb skill.

At the sharp curve just before the pits you could get a close-up view of man and car. Boillot braked, changed gear, steered, with the whole of his body in vigorous action. Man and car were one. And, as

c

G.P. de l'A.C.F. triumph, Amiens, 1913 . . .

ever the car was held to what seemed an inch on the loose stone surface
of the corner. Try hard as they did the Mercedes drivers could do no
more than hold the Peugeot; the distance between the rival cars remained
the same.

The question apparent in everyone's mind was whether the Peugeot
could stand the strain, for all the time its driver was extracting the
very last ounce of power from its engine. Certainly the one man who
could maintain the speed in such circumstances was Boillot. He knew,
and was in sympathy with, the car's mechanism. His artistry was
superb, his driving magnificent to watch.

At half distance the Peugeot and Lautenschlager's Mercedes pulled
in for a refill and wheel change. Boillot and his mechanic surpassed
themselves, so gained time over their rival. But from the moment
Lautenschlager re-started it was obvious that he was flat out to reduce
the Peugeot's lead and that he was succeeding. Almost breathless, the
crowd, quick to appreciate the situation, followed the battle. A thousand
stop watches clicked as each car came round. Nothing else in the race
mattered.

Boillot continued to put everything into this race, exceeding even
the most optimistic forecast of what he and his car could do. You could
hear the engine go right up to its maximum before every gear change,
the man was fiercely alive as was his car. Down the switchback straight
the Peugeot was no longer steady, twice at least on the hairpin bend
before the pits the car came round sideways and once there was a gasp
as the Peugeot slid right up to the far bank on the Virage de la Mort.

In comparison the Mercedes looked rock steady, holding the Peugeot
with all the inevitableness of Fate. And behind Lautenschlager were
two more cars of the German team travelling almost as fast. All else
was forgotten in the excitement of the moment.

Very near the end the Mercedes suddenly closed on the Peugeot
quite rapidly. Something was happening to France's champion. But he
could still just win. And then with only 40 miles to go out of the 466 no

. . . and tragedy, Lyon, 1914

Peugeot appeared at that corner on the hillside where first the cars could be seen from the stand. Instead white Mercedes, white Mercedes, white Mercedes.

Far away on the circuit the Peugeot had stopped with engine trouble. Boillot wept. Who could blame him? His most magnificent drive against great odds had ended wretchedly . . .

At the grandstands the three Mercedes crossed the line in absolute silence, a silence which could be felt. This was emphasized when the Goux' Peugeot came home fourth and the band played it over the line with a triumphant Marseillaise. A week or so and we were all at war. Another racing era had ended in an epic race. Its hero, Boillot, was killed in action. But whatever happens in motor racing in the future the memory of that great driver can never fade.

RALPH DE PALMA

by MERVYN KAUFMAN

HE was as much admired as he was respected by all who knew him, and his fans were a varied legion sprinkled throughout the Western Hemisphere. For Americans he was a symbol of 'up-by-the-bootstraps' industry; Italians considered him part of their folklore, even though he had left Italy as a nine-year-old in 1892 and remembered little of the mother tongue. Sportsmanship and showmanship were wedded to his nature, but the only excess of which he was perennially guilty was winning.

In twenty-seven years of racing, Ralph De Palma won more than 2,000 of the 2,800 contests he entered. He could win in any car he drove, if the fates were with him, and he could drive on board tracks and road courses with equal dexterity and *élan*.

Like many another champion, De Palma developed his obsession with speed at an early age. Growing up in Brooklyn, New York, he delivered groceries after school, thoroughly straining his patience until he had saved enough money to buy a bicycle. Then as a teenager he decided to test his skill in bicycle races, but lacking the stamina required of winners, he eventually turned to motor cycles. The most significant race of his three-year motor cycle racing career occurred at the Coney Island Driving Park. He was one of six entrants in a 10-mile race, and as he alone crossed the finish line, the judges awarded him two medals!

In 1904, at the age of 21, he saw his first motor race, the Vanderbilt Cup on Long Island. He was dazzled at once by the racing panorama —the speed, the dust, the engine noise, the crowd—and was determined to build his own racing car. Lengthy experience with bikes and motorcycles had made him an excellent mechanic; the car he assembled was the work of a virtuoso, and also a virtual catalogue of miscellania.

The car, completed in 1906, was not destined to race, however, but De Palma made a fine profit selling it to a pair of monied Princeton students. By then he was working as a mechanic for a Franklin agency in Brooklyn. He might have stayed there too, if Fred Moscovics, parts distributor who had helped him assemble the racing car, hadn't reappeared in his life. Moscovics had gone into business with Walter Allen to produce a racing car called the Allen-Kingston, and he wanted Ralph to drive it in competition.

Ralph demurred, as he had never raced a car, but Moscovics finally convinced him to enter the Fort George hill-climb of 1908, to be run in upper Manhattan. The day of the event saw De Palma, an unknown apprentice, clenching the wheel of his Allen-Kingston in confusion. At the line with him was an array of journeyman drivers including Barney Oldfield, that swaggering show-off who was to become a legend in his own right and, in a few years, De Palma's arch rival. Engine idling, Ralph awaited the starter's gun, only to be told gruffly that his front wheels had crept a few inches over the line. Obediently he backed up, just as the gun went off. He began the climb in reverse and naturally was not even placed.

After such a dismal showing, Ralph was content to take a seat at the mechanics bench in the A-K plant and remain there, but Moscovics had faith that Ralph could become a first-rate driver. Little more than a year later this faith was confirmed. De Palma began performing well for himself and also for A-K—so well, in fact, that he was lured away from Moscovics to become a driver for Fiat.

By the end of the 1909 racing season De Palma had won thirty-four races and had taken eighteen world records. And he had competed often and nobly against cigar-chewing Barney Oldfield. Although Ralph's reputation was firmly established by his performance in Fiats, his greatest glory was earned in the years he raced for Mercedes. One of his most spectacular and best-remembered races took place in 1912 at Indianapolis.

Eighty thousand spectators watched as De Palma and his co-driver Rupert Jeffkins piloted the chain-driven Number 4 Mercedes into the lead on the third lap. After a 50-mile duel their only challenger, David Bruce-Brown's National, was forced out by piston trouble and although another National, driven by Joe Dawson, was running second it was not even close. At 350 miles, De Palma was three laps ahead; at 450 he led by five laps.

As the grey Mercedes swung into the 196th lap, with but five more to go, the roar of the engine suddenly became a shrill metallic hammering. De Palma and Jeffkins were jolted out of their certainty: connecting rod failure! De Palma slowed down as a trail of white smoke poured out of his exhaust. Dawson was jolted too. Realizing that De Palma was in trouble, he began to burn rubber in earnest. Flat out, Dawson's National reduced the Mercedes' lead to four laps.

There wasn't time for a pit stop. All De Palma could do was hope for the miracle that would permit Mercedes to maintain its shrinking lead and finish the race. Within a mile of the finish line, the Mercedes engine backfired, belched one final blast of smoke and died. As far as De Palma's chances of victory were concerned, the race was over, but he couldn't just walk away from it. He ordered Jeffkins out of the car, and together they pushed the 2,000 lb. Mercedes towards the finish line.

They didn't make it, needless to say. Exhaustion and Dawson's National overtook them, but the crowd cheered them on, stirred by the display of guts and determination by a man who would tolerate defeat only on his own terms.

Mercedes Number 4 wasn't through racing. Later that year it was back at speed, as De Palma bore it to first place in the Vanderbilt Cup, Elgin National Trophy and Free-for-All races. But a crash during the American Grand Prix at Milwaukee, put De Palma into hospital for nine weeks and put the car out to pasture—permanently, it then seemed, even to Ralph.

In 1913, hired to lead the Mercer racing team, De Palma began modifying a car he planned to drive in the 1914 Vanderbilt Cup. When he learned that Barney Oldfield had also been hired to drive for Mercer, he walked out. Barney was jubilant, for life would be easier without De Palma to contend with. But Barney's joy was short lived; it became known that Ralph was more determined than ever to be in the race.

He resurrected the old grey Mercedes, and in three weeks completely reconditioned it. He trailed the pack in the early stages of the Cup race,

Worlds apart. G.P. de l'A.C.F., Dieppe, 1912 . . .

. . . and Indianapolis, 1924

but that was according to plan. Let Barney and the others burn their tyres to shreds and make pit stops; he would play a waiting game. By the thirteenth lap he had edged into second place. Then the race became a two-man contest, or a duel between titans as sports writers later described it. De Palma led Oldfield on the turns, but Barney continually surged ahead on the straights.

Ten laps to go, and Barney was slowing down a bit. The reason, Ralph could see, was that another Mercer tyre was beginning to shred. Certainly Barney would try to finish the race anyway, unless . . .

De Palma accelerated past Oldfield and signalled his pit crew that he planned to come in on the next lap. He made sure Barney saw the signal. Then he dropped back, as did Barney, who decided that as long as De Palma was stopping, he would indulge in a few stationary moments in the interest of safety. As his crew pulled off the Mercer's tyres, Ralph rolled by—bypassing his own pit—and continued on around the track. Barney had been duped, or so it seemed. De Palma hadn't planned to stop at all!

Out of the pits in a rage, Barney man-handled the Mercer through six hair-raising laps, striving to overtake the Mercedes. He was still 200 yards behind as De Palma took the chequered flag.

De Palma's urge to win was second to none, but it was equally matched by a desire to win fairly. In 1915 he was pitted against Bob Burman who had been breaking Barney Oldfield's records in Barney's discarded cars. Match races were popular then, and the site of the De Palma–Burman duel was the two-mile board speedway at Sheepshead Bay, New York. Racing four miles, De Palma in a Sunbeam, Burman in a 'Blitzen' Benz, the drivers finished in what appeared a dead heat. After a long and heated debate, the judges declared De Palma the winner —by an inch. But De Palma, silver-haired then, though only 32, overruled them. 'As we crossed the finish line,' he said, 'I was watching our front wheels. Bob was three inches in front'.

When America entered the First World War and racing activities were suspended, De Palma enlisted in the Army Air Service, learned to fly at McCook Field in Daytona, Florida. At war's end he returned to Daytona, not in a plane, but in a V-12 Packard, and driving faster than flight, average 149.887 miles per hour to set a new absolute Land Speed Record. He ran again in the French Grand Prix of 1921—he had raced one of the 14-litre Fiats in the 1912 race and a Vauxhall in 1914— and this time was placed second with a Ballot behind fellow country-man Murphy's Duesenberg.

Oldfield retired from racing at forty, but De Palma refused, defying Barney's gibes about his 'long white beard' and the snipings of some sports writers. When he was placed seventh at Indianapolis in 1925, most enthusiasts thought he was through. But less than two months later he won the 100-mile main event at Rockingham Park, New Hampshire, and in 1929 he captured the Canadian Championship.

He retired, finally, in the early 1930's and died at seventy-two in 1956, a man known for his dignity as well as his cool head, his courtesy as well as his derring-do.

The principal racing successes of **RALPH DE PALMA**

1911	2nd:	W. Vanderbilt Cup.
	3rd:	Savannah Grand Prize.
1912	1st:	Elgin Trophy; W. Vanderbilt Cup.
1913	2nd:	Indianapolis 500.
1914	1st:	Elgin Trophy; W. Vanderbilt Cup.
1915	1st:	Indianapolis 500.
1920	1st:	Elgin Trophy.
1921	2nd:	French G.P.

Tours, 1923

SIR HENRY SEGRAVE

by CYRIL POSTHUMUS

BRITISH cars and drivers have not always won Grands Prix, certainly not as inevitably as nowadays. Very far from it. The first Grand Prix of all took place in 1906; the first Grand Prix won by a British car came seventeen years later, in 1923; the second was a year after that. The driver in both cases was Henry O'Neal de Hane Segrave. Not for a further thirty-one years did another British driver in a British car win a Grand Prix; there is the measure of just some of Segrave's achievements.

Just as 'William the Conqueror, 1066' has been dinned into British heads at school, so 'French Grand Prix, 1923' comes up automatically whenever Segrave's name is mentioned. Yet that heavily chronicled victory was neither the beginning, the epitome, nor the culmination of his accomplishments. It was, indeed, a lucky win, as he frankly admitted, yet it was a true 'copybook' Segrave success as he himself advocated. He did not believe in ten-tenths racing; 'never go faster than you have to to control the opposition' he counselled.

The story of the classic race at Tours is well known. Three 'hush-hush' supercharged Fiats set a staggering pace, chased hard by Kenelm Lee Guinness in one Sunbeam while Segrave in another lay further back, his 'take it steady at first' policy enforced by a slipping clutch. The Fiats dropped out one by one, Guinness's car lost a vital gear, and Segrave, his clutch suddenly 'repairing itself' when a pedal obstruction broke free, went through to win for Sunbeam and for Britain.

He won many other race victories during his career, but that one had the greatest impact. Yet though he admired success above all things ('I'd rather sit next to Henry Ford at dinner than anyone else in the world' he once said) his Tours win never went to his head. It was simply the climax of his fervent ambition to become a racing driver. Many young people have this ambition, but few have the dogged determination to pursue it against all odds. Graham Hill is probably today's classic example; Segrave is yesterday's.

Descending from an old Leicestershire family, and son of an Irish-domiciled father and an American mother, Henry Segrave left Eton when war broke out in 1914 to become an infantry officer at 18. He served in the trenches until 1915, then joined the Royal Flying Corps, was shot down by anti-aircraft fire, broke an ankle, and had to have several silver plates in his foot to be able to walk again. Invalided out of active warfare, he joined the executive side of the Air Ministry, went to the United States as attaché to an aviation mission, and was there when the Armistice was signed.

While in the States he became friends with Bill Bruce-Brown, brother of the famous American driver. They talked racing, and Segrave visited the Sheepshead Bay track on Long Island, to acquire an engraved plaque for lapping at 82 m.p.h. in his Apperson touring car.

Thus did he get his first severe bites from the 'speed bug' and, being a man of action, a 'go-getter', he lost no time when back home again in asking Louis Coatalen, chief of the Anglo-French Sunbeam-Talbot-Darracq racing team, for a place in it.

Not surprisingly the answer was 'No'. Then Segrave invested some money in a Knightsbridge garage owning two 1914 Grand Prix Opels, bought one, and raced it at Brooklands. In his very first race, at Whitsun in 1920, he gained fame in an unexpected way—a rear tyre flew off the Opel at over 100 m.p.h., but he held the car skilfully, and three-quarters of an hour later won his second race in the same car. That put his name in the newspapers, and with plentiful ammunition in headlines from *The Times*, *Daily Chronicle* and the *Daily Telegraph*, Segrave again approached Coatalen.

Again the answer was 'No'. He won two more races in August, and took three seconds and three thirds during the rest of the season. Still Coatalen said 'No', but he was wavering before the clear blue eyes and sincere, eager face of this tall and obviously talented young man. And when an S.T.D. team entry of four cars for the 1921 French G.P. was announced, Segrave drove straight up to Coatalen in Wolverhampton and again fired the question.

The Patron yielded at last—Segrave could have the fourth car, but he must meet his own expenses and pay for any damage to the car. And if he finished, there might be a permanent place in the team for him. As a try-out Segrave drove a prototype G.P. Sunbeam at Brooklands on Easter Monday, 1921, winning his race with ease. Then he went into hard training for the Grand Prix; no drinking, which didn't worry him, for he disliked alcohol, and no smoking, which he found hard. So did his colleagues, from whom 'non-smoker' Segrave scrounged cigarette after cigarette at times of stress!

It proved a gruelling race for him. On the very rough circuit he had to change tyres fourteen times, his oil tank was holed by a flying stone, his mechanic knocked out by another, the ignition timing slipped, the

Road racing. Fulfilment, G.P. de l'A.C.F., 1923 . . .

car persistently overheated, and finished the race on six of its eight cylinders, ninth and last, but a *finisher*. 'I think, if the engine had fallen into two pieces, or one of the axles had cracked, I would somehow have succeeded in finishing' said Segrave. 'To get there meant more than anything in the world to me'.

He got his place in the S.T.D. team, and four months later won his first major event, the 200-Miles Race at Brooklands. Ambition and push had got him so far, but such was the irony of racing that, in his second season, and apart from short Brooklands track events, Segrave did not win a single race though he broke the T.T. lap record and was second in the Sicilian Coppa Florio. But he gained invaluable experience to enrich his racing philosophy. 'It is always the winner who is believed to have the most trying time,' he wrote feelingly 'but in reality it is incomparably more trying to have to struggle to carry on with a car that is crocked in order to finish at all'.

Nineteen-twenty-three and the glory of Tours amply compensated, and two months later Segrave won another race—the Boulogne G.P. des Voiturettes with a Talbot-Darracq. In 1924 he lost the French G.P. through magneto trouble on his Sunbeam, but with the same supercharged 2-litre car he won the Spanish G.P. at San Sebastian with such expertise that one local paper was moved to comment '*Segrave won with a master hand; he seemed to have in his head from start to finish a timetable. . . . He is El Maestro Completo*'. It was, in fact, a model 'Segrave' win; the roads were treacherous with rain and sticky clay, his gearing prevented him from ever using top gear, but he made no mistakes, kept the opposition nicely under control, and like a Caracciola, Moss, Fangio or Clark, won as he wished without needless risks.

At the end of that year Segrave became a paid and therefore truly professional driver, employed by Sunbeams as London sales chief and works driver. His experience showed in other ways than more victories; with S. C. H. ('Sammy') Davis he pioneered the use of the now universally worn crash helmet; he secured fairer bonuses and *primes* for drivers, and in general did much to gain recognition for them as performers worthy of their cost, many benefits he fought for being passed down to today's drivers.

And he continued to win races—the 1925 and 1926 200-Miles Races at Brooklands, the 1925 and 1926 G.P.s de Provence at Miramas, 1925 Shelsley Walsh and Kop hill-climbs, races at Southport, speed trials at Boulogne and Blackpool. . . . When he stopped racing early in 1927, the greatest star of his decade, Segrave had secured thirty-one firsts out of forty-nine events. He then turned to wholly speed records. He had, in fact, started to take an interest in this aspect of the sport in 1926 when with the V-12 4-litre Sunbeam he broke the World's Land Speed Record on Southport sands at 152·33 m.p.h. He held it for six weeks only, when Parry Thomas took it away.

His next effort, a year later, was a masterpiece of persuasion and shoestring improvisation by Segrave and Coatalen. Sunbeams were hard up, yet recognized the publicity value of breaking the world land speed record, not by a few m.p.h. but by a decisive margin. The resultant '1,000-h.p.' Sunbeam used two old First World War Matabele aero-engines, chain drive, and the first all-enveloping streamlined body. Segrave was to drive the monster but, more than that, had to organize the entire project and canvass for sponsors.

. . . Disappointment, G.P. de l'A.C.F., 1924

His great charm, drive and persuasive powers took him through, but when he insisted that only Daytona beach in Florida, U.S.A., was suitable for the record attack, he had to take on the responsibility, planning and expense of the journey himself. It was a big gamble, but his confidence was richly justified in March 1927 when he broke the record at 203·79 m.p.h. and became even more of a national hero.

Then he left Sunbeams to join the Portland Cement Co. as a director, sales executive and concrete roads expert, one condition being 'no more racing'. He didn't mind; Grand Prix racing was in an unhappy phase, and motorboat racing had now caught his interest instead, first with outboard dinghies with which he did well at Hythe and Kew, then with a bigger Chris-Craft hydroplane with which he won at Hythe in 1928. Ever versatile, he also plunged into car body design, producing the handsome Hillman 'Segrave' coupé, drove his own 45-h.p. Renault from San Sebastian to Paris at an average of 57 m.p.h., and wrote his book *The Lure of Speed* and numerous articles.

Then first Malcolm Campbell and next the Americans broke his world record, and Segrave resolved to get it back. A new car, the Napier Lion-engined 'Golden Arrow' was built, backed by numerous sponsors including two directors of the Portland Cement Co.—such were the Segrave powers of persuasion! He took the car to Daytona early in 1929, together with a new Napier-engined racing boat called 'Miss England'. On March 11 he broke the L.S.R. at 231·36 m.p.h., beating the old figure by over 23 m.p.h., and ten days later, in *Miss England*, he beat Gar Wood's 2,200-h.p. *Miss America V* in the Fischer Cup race at Biscayne, Miami.

Returning to England on the *Olympic* he received a telegram advising him that he was to be knighted for his achievements. His homecoming reception was tremendous; he was the man of the hour, a true knight of speed, but it never affected his balance nor his charm, nor his relentless drive forward. He took *Miss England* to Potsdam and won the German Water Championships, then to Venice to win the European Championship and the Volpi Cup. Always interested in aircraft, he left the Portland Cement Co. to become technical adviser to the newly-formed Aircraft Investment Corporation, and co-designed a new light twin-engined monoplane called the Segrave Meteor. He lent his name to a new sparking-plug, took on new directorships, designed another Hillman Segrave car, and then announced a new £25,000 *Miss England II*, to attack the absolute water speed record.

It was to have two Rolls-Royce aero-engines, jointly giving over 3,000 h.p., and over 115 m.p.h. was expected. The aim was high and the boat complex, but Sir Henry's iron will smoothed out troubles one by one until, on Friday the 13th of June, he set out on Lake Windermere to attack America's 92·86 m.p.h. World Water Speed Record. Without incident the outward and return runs were accomplished, and by his stopwatch Segrave knew that the record had been easily broken. He was never to know the exact figure (98·76 m.p.h.) for on a third run, flat out to see if he could exceed 120 m.p.h., the boat struck an obstruction in the water, pitched over at full speed, and sank in a terrible flurry of spray and steam.

Struck at over 100 m.p.h. water is like concrete, and his unofficial speed on that run was 119·8 m.p.h. One riding engineer was killed instantly, the other, Michael Wilcocks, lived to tell the awful story. Sir Henry Segrave was taken from the water with both arms broken,

Against the clock. Boulogne, 1925 . . .

. . . being pushed off at Southport, 1926

a crushed thigh, broken ribs and head injuries; two and a half hours later he died of a haemorrhage through a perforated lung.

Later that year the ashes of Britain's greatest speed exponent of the first half of the twentieth century were taken up by his father, Charles Segrave, in the Segrave Meteor monoplane, and scattered over the playing fields of Eton. A few weeks before, he said to a friend, 'If I go out, may it be doing something worth while. God save me from dying between the sheets'. He had gone out as he wished.

The principal racing successes of **SIR HENRY SEGRAVE**

1921	1st:	J.C.C. 200.		2nd:	G.P. de l'Ouverture, Montlhéry.
	3rd:	Le Mans Voiturette Race.		3rd:	J.C.C. 200.
1922	2nd:	Coppa Florio.	1925	1st:	Provence G.P.; J.C.C. 200.
	3rd:	Le Mans Voiturette Race; J.C.C. 200.		3rd:	G.P. de l'Ouverture, Montlhéry.
1923	1st:	French G.P.; G.P. des Voiturettes, Boulogne.	1926	1st:	Provence G.P.; J.C.C. 200.
1924	1st:	San Sebastian G.P.		2nd:	G.P. du Salon, Montlhéry.

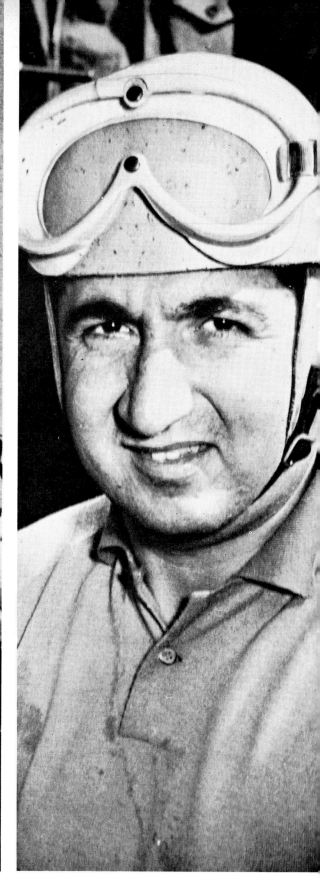

Antonio Ascari

Alberto Ascari

ANTONIO AND ALBERTO ASCARI

by GIANNI CANCELLIERI

THE drama-packed careers of the Ascaris are tragically engraved in the annals of motor racing—Antonio and Alberto, father and son, both died at the wheel of a racing car, thirty years one from the other, after both had ruled the international racing scene . . .

Antonio was born on September 15, 1888 in Bonferraro di Sorgà, a tiny clustered village at the edge of the Verona province, quite near the Mantuan border, and a stone's throw from Castel d'Ario, the village in which four years later Tazio Nuvolari was to see the light of day.

Antonio only spent his childhood days in his native borough, in the mild, damp, green plain which Shakespeare made runaway Romeo cross when 'banished from the world'. He was only a youth when, at the beginning of the century, he moved with his family to Milan, the town which, together with Turin and Genoa, was then leading the tardy but earnest Italian industrial revolution. Apprentice bicycle mechanic at first, apprentice car mechanic later, he finally got a job at the De Vecchi workshop, where the cars bearing that name were constructed.

At that time motoring was still taking its first awkward but vigorous steps and Antonio was soon fascinated by it, and by its sporting side. For a long time he could brood only about this new passion, and was able to indulge in it only in April, 1911, in the Modena 'Six Days' (an endurance event); De Vecchi, where he had in the meantime become a foreman, entered him with a works car. Although his début was not crowned with success, he did show the qualities for which he was to become outstanding, first among them a capacity for understanding mechanism, which fact enabled him to handle the car very effectively coupled to a spectacular, even acrobatic, style.

However, the De Vecchi firm was short-lived and Ascari therefore joined ALFA, soon to become Alfa Romeo, as a test driver. His racing activity came therefore to a sudden, compulsory standstill which the First World War was to extend along the years.

However, rather than cooling down, his passion smouldered and eventually exploded once more with renewed vigour. In 1919 Antonio attended a race, which Giuseppe Campari won, on the Cremona circuit. Ascari accosted the winner immediately after the race, congratulated him and in effect challenged him by saying, 'I can drive like that'. 'Maybe,' was Campari's answer.

It can be said that Ascari's short but glorious career started at that moment. He bought a 4·5-litre Fiat which had been built for Indianapolis (but never raced there) and was immediately successful, winning the classic Italian hill-climbs of those times, Parma-Poggio di Berceto and the Coppa della Consuma. Then he crashed in the Targa Florio and was out of racing for nearly two years.

In 1921 he became a sales agent for Alfa Romeo and took part, with ever-growing enthusiasm, in the foremost Italian events, gaining a hill-climb victory at Surgagno and then finishing fourth in the Targa

Fiat-mounted for the 1919 Parma-Poggio di Berceto hill-climb

39

Florio. He became a works driver for the Portello firm, joining Giuseppe Campari and Ugo Sivocci, and soon acquiring great popularity.

In 1924 Antonio Ascari 'arrived'. On the extremely fast Cremona circuit—where he had won in the previous year with a 3-litre Alfa—he first appeared with the brand new Alfa Romeo P.2; a legendary future was awaiting both man and car. In his first race outside Italy he led the French G.P. at Lyons until with two laps to go his engine failed (his team-mate won); he had seemed to have the Targa Florio in his pocket when within 50 yards of the finish his engine seized. But in the autumn of the same year Ascari led the Alfa Romeo team in their Italian G.P. victory at Monza, covering 497 miles at 98·79 m.p.h., a speed which it is hardly necessary to underline.

Driving the irresistible P.2, Ascari scored an overwhelming victory in the European G.P. on the Spa-Francorchamps circuit in the early summer of 1925 and seemed all set for an outstanding season.

It was therefore as a great driver, the driver of the day, that Ascari leapt immediately into the lead in the G.P. de l'A.C.F., held on the Montlhéry track on July 26, 1925. After 150 very fast miles he led by four minutes. Then, suddenly, a crash: coming out of a wide radius, slightly uphill corner on a track slippery with light rain, Ascari grazed a fence with the hub of a front wheel and lost control of the car, which at the time was travelling at about 110 m.p.h. The car was hurled against the fence, uprooting posts which gathered under it, and then spun down the track, throwing out its fatally injured driver.

There were many conjectures and surmises on the causes of the misfortune: some thought the driver might have suffered a sudden collapse, other spoke of a possible driver error, even hinted at foul play. But it does seem that wire from the pale fencing by the track entwined itself

Before his last race, Montlhéry, 1925

around a hub and locked the wheel, making the driver finally lose control of the car.

Antonio Ascari died on his way from the track to the hospital. When news of his death was heard, Alfa Romeo, for whom Campari was still leading the race, withdrew their team as a sign of mourning . . .

He left a widow, a daughter and a son, Alberto, born on July 13, 1918 and thus just seven years old. He was left with the image of his father as a simple and loving man of athletic build, who always took him to his nearly daily practice in Monza, sometimes letting him ride at his side in the cars he drove; an image which embodied the spirit of daring, of vigour, of skill, and which infused an unconquerable sense of protection and safety, yet did not fade without imbuing Alberto with an indefinite eagerness to emulate.

He was eleven years old when he jumped on the saddle of a neighbour's motor cycle and went to 'race' in the large square usually used for military parades. From that day his mother, poor Signora Eliza, began fearing for his life. She put him in school but studying was not quite Alberto's cup of tea. At least he did study, but only all the possible expedients which could enable him to make money and save it with a sole aim: to hire a motor cycle and rush off to Monza and 'practise'. It was only possible to realize this aim during the holidays and when these were no longer sufficient Alberto decided to multiply them. He escaped from one school after the other and his mother was adamant, just shutting him up once more, but always more dispiritedly till, finally, one day she gave up.

The year was 1936. Alberto was not quite 18 and having escaped from school for the umpteenth time, he rang his mother up from Milan station, to announce that 'he just wanted to race motor cycles'.

With the proceeds from the sale of his gold chronograph, with his schoolboy savings—and helped also by a tangible contribution from his mother—Alberto bought his first motor cycle, a 500-c.c. Sertum.

With this, on June 28, 1936, he made his first sporting appearance in a 24-hour regularity test across northern Italy. His début, as was his father's, was unfortunate: he had two falls, the second of which (near Pisa) definitely ended his run, as Alberto spun at a corner when his rear brake failed and he retired in a tomato field. However, six days later, when he had repaired his machine, he tasted the salt of victory by winning his class in a regularity test on the Lario circuit.

By now his mother was resigned. Many years later, Alberto himself declared, during an interview: 'In a certain sense she had got used to the atmosphere of racing. My father had trained her, one might say'. However, from the day that his dreams began to come true, the son did his best to gain forgiveness by taking a serious interest in his mother's shop and by striving to 'undramatize' his life always maintaining that he considered nothing more than his 'trade'.

In the privacy of his home, at first with his mother then with his wife and children, he rarely spoke of drivers, engines and races, just as an office clerk rarely mentions his muddle of papers, his colleagues and his boss. His home itself was witness of this peculiar aspect of this character for it bore not even the faintest resemblance to the 'sanctuary home' of many drivers. There was a large bust of his father in the hall, but nothing else. Cups, trophies and relics of all kinds were almost bashfully hidden in a discreet crystal cabinet.

In 1937 the 18-year-old Alberto continued his career on two wheels and made his début in speed events, gaining five victories, three second placings and, at the end of the season, a contract with Bianchi. In the next two years of motor cycle racing he was far from unsuccessful, but Alberto was getting a stronger urge to switch from two to four wheels, to emulate the two Italian aces of these days, Nuvolari and Varzi, who had both been motor cyclists before turning to cars. Moreover, only at the wheel of a car would he be able to follow in his father's footsteps.

Exempt from military duty in the Spring of 1940 (by now he was owner of a concern which transported fuel to North Africa) Alberto made his first race appearance, on April 28, in the closed-circuit Mille Miglia of that year. He drove a 1·5-litre eight cylinder Ferrari 815, the first model created by the 'Commendatore' and was leading in his category when he was obliged to retire, owing to valve failure. With a Maserati 6CM he then gained ninth place in the Tripoli Grand Prix and then retired once more in the Targa Florio. Within the next few days Alberto's pre-war career was to end.

Ascari still wasn't called up—owing to the enterprise already mentioned—even after Italy entered the war. He got married and later had to flee in the Val d'Aosta woods to avoid being caught by German search parties. When the war ended, Ascari was 27 years old, he had a wife and a son (Antonio jr. nicknamed 'Tonino', born in 1942, who, by the mid-sixties, was also racing single-seaters, albeit without the single-mindedness of his grandfather and father), a business which had to be put on its feet again and—as he himself said one day—'a mother whom I wanted to have as peaceful an old age as possible'.

However, it wasn't long before 'Ciccio' once more took up the wheel of a car. Villoresi, who had helped him take his first steps in the racing world, convinced him that he should return to it. So on September 28, 1947 Alberto Ascari scored his first victory in a car race, driving a Maserati at Modena. From that day his career rose towards the heights —works driver for Ferrari in 1949, Champion of Italy, World Champion in 1952 and 1953.

In his first full season, he won the San Remo Grand Prix and the Pescara Sports Car Race and was runner-up to his mentor Villoresi in the British Grand Prix. For Ferrari in 1949 he won at Bari, Berne, Rheims and Silverstone; in his Maserati he scored at Buenos Aires. And so on to the year of the 2-litre Grands Prix. In his first championship year, 1952, he won the Belgian, British, Dutch, German and Italian Grands Prix; in 1953 the Argentine, Belgian, British, Dutch and Swiss Grands Prix fell to him.

Undoubtedly Alberto was an exceptional champion. His handling of the car was completely natural, at times light and flowing, at times vigorous and determined, dictated by a prodigious, instinctive, dynamic sensitiveness. Furthermore, to his stylistic precision and to the promptness of his reflexes was coupled an innate tactical shrewdness—one recalls the well-known episode at the Nürburgring, when, two laps from the end of the race he was 42 seconds ahead of Fangio, stopped at the pits to change tyres, restarting with a meagre advantage and holding it to the end.

Ascari was a basically good man and had a sparkling personality. In racing circles everywhere he was liked and respected: 'One of the most admirable traits of his character was his generous appreciation of other drivers' skill'—his obituary in *The Times* recalled.

After gaining his second world title, Ascari left Ferrari. 'I needed the kind of financial security dear old Ferrari couldn't give me,' explained Ascari. To which the 'Commendatore' replied: 'If one wants to keep one's friends, one must never ask them for too great favours. I want to go on being Alberto's friend'.

Ascari then went to Lancia and with one of their sports cars at last managed to win the Mille Miglia (1954) but as regards Formula 1 he had to bide his time. His day seemed to dawn in the Spring of 1955, but darkness was soon to engulf it.

Death came to Ascari just when he was once more trying to get to the top in Grand Prix racing. On March 27, 1955, in Turin's Valentino Grand Prix, he gained for the Torinese firm its first victory in a F.1 event; on May 9, in winning the Naples G.P. he showed how sound were his aspirations towards the 'great comeback'. In relationship to the brand-new Italian car he was in a curiously similar position to that which his father had occupied *vis-à-vis* the Alfa Romeo P.2 exactly thirty years earlier and both machines had been designed by the same brilliant engineer, Vittorio Jano. (The coincidences of detail, of minutiae, during the final vicissitudes of both the Ascaris are many and constitute a sort of macabre puzzle around their tragic deaths.)

The last week of Alberto's life began at Monaco. On the eighty-first lap of the European Grand Prix the last of the Mercedes fell out and as he was about to inherit the lead, 'Ciccio' shot down to the chicane, his front right wheel locked and he was flung into the harbour at a speed of 100 m.p.h. When he was fished out of the water his condition was not too bad: his nose and back were bruised and he was slightly shocked.

Back in Milan on May 26, four days after the accident, Ascari was not fully recovered, but wanted to take some exercise! So he went down to Monza where on that Thursday practice for the 1000 km Supercortemaggiore sports car race—from which he had already withdrawn —was going on. The Ferrari clan—to whom his memory remains imperishable—greeted him with a friendly show of affection and esteem, and who could deny his request to try a car? 'Ciccio' started. One lap, two laps, then the end. Having passed through Lesmo's second curve and on entering the one which is now known as Curva Ascari, he suddenly braked. The 3-litre Ferrari slithered on the asphalt, spun from the track, reared, rolled and threw its driver some twenty-five yards.

Poor 'Ciccio' died in the ambulance which was taking him to Monza hospital, thirty years after his father had died in an ambulance between Montlhéry and Paris. Both were 36 years old when they died, both accidents happened on the 26th of the month and the full circumstances of both have never been, and perhaps never will be, completely cleared up.

Alberto's accident gave rise to similar surmises: the driver might have been at fault (as a consequence of the Monaco shock) or suffered a seizure (just before, at the pits, he had been seen eating a couple of sandwiches) but it seemed obvious that he had desperately braked to avoid something or someone. Who? A deer has been suggested, a workman has been mentioned—coming from the brickyard of the high-speed oval which was being built at the time, he was said to have reached the edge of the road circuit and started to cross it just as Ascari's car was arriving. Inevitably, part of the Press didn't hesitate to give credit to this version of the accident, far-fetched as it may sound; it was even said that the workman's identity is known and that

New driver, new marque. Alberto waiting in his Ferrari to start in the 1940 Mille Miglia . . .

. . . and before his last race, Monaco, 1955

4·5 Ferrari, San Remo, 1951 . . .

at present he is interned in an asylum near Milan, victim of the conse-quences of the appalling psychic trauma.

True or not, any attempt to reconstruct the accident is of little consequence. The truth is that in losing Alberto Ascari, Italy lost the greatest upholder of what was perhaps her most radiant sporting tradition. 'Ciccio's' death created such a void that, even after ten years, it is still impossible to see who may fill it.

Lancia, 1954 Mille Miglia

... 2·0 Ferrari, Belgian Grand Prix, 1953

The principal racing successes of **ANTONIO ASCARI**

1923	1st:	Cremona Circuit.
	2nd:	Targa Florio.
	3rd:	Circuit of Mugello.
1924	1st:	Italian G.P.; Cremona Circuit.
	2nd:	Italian Touring Car G.P.
1925	1st:	European G.P.

The principal racing successes of **ALBERTO ASCARI**

1947	1st:	Modena Sports Car Race.
	2nd:	Cairo Cisitalia Marque Race.
1948	1st:	Pescara G.P.; San Remo G.P.
	2nd:	British G.P.
	3rd:	French G.P.
1949	1st:	Italian G.P.; Swiss G.P.; International Trophy, Silverstone; Coupe des Petites Cylindrées, Rheims; Bari G.P.; Peron G.P., Buenos Aires.
	2nd:	Lausanne G.P.
	3rd:	Belgian G.P.; Autodrome G.P., Monza; Rosario G.P.
1950	1st:	German G.P.; Coupe des Petites Cylindrées, Rheims; Mons G.P.; Penya Rhin G.P.; Circuit of Garda; Modena G.P.; Rome G.P.; Luxembourg G.P.; Peron G.P., Buenos Aires; Mar del Plata G.P.
	2nd:	Italian G.P.; Monaco G.P.; Marseilles G.P.; Autodrome G.P., Monza.
	3rd:	Dutch G.P.
1951	1st:	German G.P.; Italian G.P.; Modena G.P.; Autodrome G.P., Monza; Naples G.P.; San Remo G.P.
	2nd:	Belgian G.P.; French G.P.; Carrera Panamericana.
1952	1st:	Belgian G.P.; British G.P.; Dutch G.P.; French G.P.; German G.P.; Italian G.P.; Comminges G.P.; la Baule G.P.; Marseilles G.P.; Pau G.P.; Syracuse G.P.
	3rd:	Rheims G.P.; Modena G.P.
1953	1st:	Argentine G.P.; Belgian G.P.; British G.P.; Dutch G.P.; Swiss G.P.; Bordeaux G.P.; Pau G.P.; Nürburgring 1000 km.
	2nd:	Casablanca 12 Hours.
1954	1st:	Mille Miglia.
1955	1st:	Naples G.P.; Valentino G.P.

After the R.A.C. Grand Prix, Brooklands, 1927

ROBERT BENOIST

by W. F. BRADLEY

ROBERT BENOIST was a country lad endowed by nature with a passion for mechanics. The tiny hamlet of Auffargis, in which he was born in March 1895, stands on the edge of the great Rambouillet forest and joins the vast Versailles domains. As a child he knew little of town life, but he was an early student of nature, his perception became remarkably quick and even in his teens he was recognized as one of the best shots of the district—a quality which was to be of immense value to him in later life.

Motor cars were becoming less uncommon in the early years of the century, but as the cost of even the cheapest would have been greater than that of the whole Benoist homestead, Robert had to be satisfied with a bicycle; with this he won a few prizes in local club events. Schooldays over, he was apprenticed to a garage proprietor in Versailles, at a time when the garage mechanic was expected to do everything from inflating a tyre to scraping main bearings.

War came while he was still enrolled as an apprentice, and in 1915 he was called up for active service as an infantryman. To his immense delight he was transferred to the Flying Corps and taught to pilot a Maurice Farman biplane; in 1917 (when he was serving on the Verdun front as a Sergeant-Pilot) he was further delighted to be given a new type machine, a Morane-Parasol, which had been sent up to the squadron. After surviving a between-the-lines crash-landing—Benoist and his observer crawled to safety while the enemy turned their guns on what was left of the machine—he flew other modern machines (Nieuports and Spads) in action. Then came a period of training at the Pau aerobatic school and in August 1919 he was discharged from the Army with 19,500 flying hours to his credit.

Benoist found his own solution to the problem of finding post-war employment by offering to drive the newly-produced de Marcay 1100 cyclecar in the 1921 Paris-to-Nice trial. This event was more of a reliability test than a race, but acceleration tests at Grenoble, a flying kilometre on the Promenade des Anglais at Nice, and the La Turbie hill-climb added to its sporting interest.

His performance was sufficiently good for him to apply for, and be granted, a place on the Salmson racing team. This firm, specializing in aero engines, had taken up light car construction and, under the management of M. Lombard, had a racing section handling the machines built to the designs of the clever engineer Emile Petit.

In 1922 the Paris municipal authorities authorized the use of the Avenue des Acacias, the main avenue running through the Bois de Boulogne, for speed trials. Benoist, driving a two-seater 1100-c.c. Salmson, made the fastest time of the day with an average of 83 m.p.h. for the flying kilometre.

After two years with Salmson, during which he took part in a variety

47

of events for 1100-c.c. cyclecars, notably the Bol d'Or 24-hour race in the Forest of St. Germain, the *équipe* was dissolved and Benoist was offered a drive with the Delage racing team.

From the days when he assembled cars one by one with De Dion Bouton single-cylinder engines, Louis Delage had been a strong believer in the value of racing. In 1924, when Benoist was enrolled, the team had just been reorganized—it had been discovered that the chief engineer intended to move to a rival firm and take all the drawings with him. Counter-measures were put into effect and, after some hesitation, it was decided that M. Lory should be nominated chief engineer of the racing department. Lory was young; his highest responsibilities had been those of chief draughtsman. It was therefore agreed that on all matters of importance he should consult the race drivers—Thomas, Benoist, Divo, Morel and Bourlier, and that M. Louis Delage should have general oversight.

Benoist's first outings with Delage were in hill-climbs with the 'big Six'. At Mont Agel, Mont Ventoux, Laffrey and Limonest he clipped seconds off the existing records. Under the able coaching of René Thomas he finished third with the 2-litre car in the 1924 French (and European) Grand Prix.

In 1925 Benoist won his first Grand Prix, driving the 12-cylinder 2-litre Delage at Montlhéry. This was a tough race—the Italian champion Ascari crashed and was killed while in the lead and it finished in drenching rain; Benoist trailed, well down the field, in the early stages but took the lead before half-distance to finish ahead of his team-mate Wagner. After this first French win in the G.P. de l'A.C.F. since 1913, Benoist and his co-driver, Divo, had the honour of being officially received by the President of the Republic.

In a Salmson, J.C.C. 200 Miles, Brooklands, 1922 . . .

The 1927 season stands out as the most brilliant in Robert Benoist's career. When it closed he was World Champion, with four firsts, in the French Grand Prix at Montlhéry, Spanish Grand Prix at San Sebastian, European Grand Prix at Monza, and the British Grand Prix organized at Brooklands by the Royal Automobile Club. All these had been won on the 1500-c.c. supercharged Delage, undoubtedly the most successful model ever produced by Lory.

In 1928 Louis Delage had so far over-stretched his financial resources that he was obliged not only to close his racing department but to sell his factory piece-meal to avoid going before the bankruptcy court. He eventually succeeded in paying all his creditors 'twenty-shillings in the pound' only to find himself so completely ruined that he had to accept a starvation salary in a hastily-formed Delahaye-Delage organization.

Thus Robert Benoist, undoubtedly the most brilliant French driver in the 'between-two-wars' period, found himself without a job.

An attempt in the Le Mans 24-hour Race with an Itala was not very successful. Then he drove a few times for Alfa Romeo and succeeded in coming home first in the Spa Grand Prix of 1928.

Then Benoist joined Bugatti in 1929, primarily as manager of the Paris sales organization, in the Avenue Montagne, and supervisor of racing activities. In 1934 he led the official Bugatti team in the French Grand Prix held at Montlhéry. Chiron won this Alfa Romeo triumph; Benoist was flagged-off fourth (and last) and a few weeks later secured the same position in the Belgian Grand Prix.

There was little racing for the Bugatti *équipe* in 1936 and Benoist busied himself with organizing class records for various distances up to six hours, all of them on Montlhéry track. In 1937, however, he was to succeed in his greatest ambition and win the Le Mans 24-hour Race. Two cars, the famous 57s, were prepared—with Benoist and J. P. Wimille and Veyron and Labric as drivers. During the second hour the two Bugattis took the lead. On the Sunday morning, after a night under heavy rain, one had to be withdrawn while in second position, but the second car, driven by Benoist and Wimille, had the race well in hand and finished at the record average of 84·5 m.p.h. It was Benoist's last race.

When the war clouds formed in September 1938, Benoist was once again called up for military service. The threat seemed to pass over and he returned to civilian life. A year later he was back in uniform but to his immense disgust he found that military regulations decreed that at 44 he was too old to fly.

In 1940 the great exodus before the invading German armies began. In his '57S' Benoist started from Le Bourget for a destination in the south-west. But even a supercharged Bugatti was no faster than a bicycle on such traffic-congested roads. The roar of sirens indicated that a German armoured column was about to rush through. In common with others, Benoist sought to get as far off the road as possible, but his unusual car attracted the attention of the officer in charge of the column who, drawing his revolver, announced that the Frenchman was his prisoner. Benoist was told to remain at the wheel; and with a sidecar outfit with machine gun following him joined the column as it moved on towards the Spanish frontier. Early the following morning Benoist found himself standing, still with the machine gun in his rear, opposite a cross roads. With the rapidity of which only a race driver

. . . and a Delage, Targa Florio, 1926

was capable, he started the Bugatti and dashed into the side road, knowing that if he could reach the bend before the machine gun went into action there was nothing in the German army capable of catching him. The attempt succeeded. That evening the Bugatti was in a safe hiding-place and Benoist had joined his unit.

When war was declared, a prominent member of the Bugatti team, known as Williams, appeared in uniform as Captain William Grover, of the Intelligence Corps. With the fall of France the Captain changed to 'civvies', grew a thick black beard and wore coloured glasses which only seemed to accentuate his disguise. Except that it had some connection with the Resistance, his friends did not know (and did not want to know) exactly what work Williams was performing. Then he disappeared. How, when, where he was captured, to what prison he was taken, was a mystery.

Benoist immediately took over his work with devouring activity, supervising the dropping of armed supplies, arranging their distribution among the Resistance groups, making frequent trips to London and returning to be parachuted into the fields he knew so well. He seemed to lead a charmed life, being captured and escaping so repeatedly and under such dramatic circumstances that one began to believe, with him, 'that they really are too stupid'.

However, he was eventually captured. But while being driven through Paris in a Gestapo car, with a guard to his right, another on his left, and third beside the driver, Benoist stretched out his arms behind the two Germans, as if to give them more room, until his fingers fell on the two leather straps which, as he knew, gave remote control of the door catches. As they were about to enter the Rue Richelieu, Benoist jerked. The doors flew open, the glass broke, the driver braked fiercely, throwing the two guards forward. Benoist assisted them in this movement then, jumping over their bodies, disappeared into the midst of a startled crowd. That evening he took the train to Brittany; the next morning he reported in London.

Back in Paris, and on his way to a secret meeting in the Avenue Hoche, Benoist realized that he was being shadowed. Climbing the staircase, he knew that the Gestapo would be waiting for him when he descended. But he also knew that by passing through a skylight he could scramble over a dozen roofs until he reached a building far removed from his point of departure. As he looked down, Benoist saw the enemy assembling for his arrest. Stopped by the concierge of the new building, Benoist gave his name and told what he was doing. Telling him to wait, the guardian explored the surrounding streets, then seeing nothing suspicious, gave the all-clear signal. Again Robert Benoist had slipped through the Germans' hands.

Driving a light van, fitted with a charcoal-gas producer and a false floor under which ammunition and documents were concealed, Benoist was stopped by Feld-Gendarmerei and ordered to proceed to headquarters for a search. In monosyllables and the use of slang, the men aboard the van agreed that their only hope lay in wrecking the van and rushing for safety. They succeeded and although one of the team was captured, he was able to convince the police that he was being given a lift and knew nothing of the others.

In 1944 came the successful Normandy landings; the Allies were breaking through and Benoist and his companions knew that the occupation was nearing its end. On June 18, 1944, entering his new

After his last race — with Wimille at Le Mans, 1937

quarters near the Ecole Militaire, he found the German police in possession. He had been betrayed. Taken first to the Gestapo torture chambers in the Avenue Foch, he refused to speak. Then came Fresnes prison and more tortures. Finally, on August 17, 1944, the 'Benoist Group' composed of thirty-six French, English, Belgian and Canadian officers, reached Buchenwald. On the night of September 12, 1944, it was ordered that they should be executed by the cruel method of slow strangulation. The second man to be killed in this hideous manner was Captain Robert Benoist, patriot, French racing driver, World Champion.

The principal racing successes of **ROBERT BENOIST**

1922	1st:	Cyclecar G.P.
	2nd:	Bol d'Or.
1923	1st:	Bol d'Or; Boulogne Voiturette G.P.; Milan Cyclecar G.P.; Spanish Voiturette G.P.
	2nd:	Voiturette G.P.
1924	3rd:	French G.P.
1925	1st:	French G.P.
	2nd:	San Sebastian G.P.
1926	3rd:	Spanish G.P.; R.A.C. G.P.
1927	1st:	French G.P.; Italian G.P.; Spanish G.P.; R.A.C. G.P.; G.P. de l'Ouverture, Montlhéry.
1928	2nd:	San Sebastian G.P.
1929	1st:	Spa 24-hour Race.
1935	1st:	Picardy G.P.
1936	2nd:	Marne G.P.
1937	1st:	Le Mans 24-hour Race.

TAZIO NUVOLARI

by JOHN EASON GIBSON

The Great Little Man

HE drove with ardour and passion but it was not just because of this that race followers, who had never been close to him, loved and admired the great little man; it was largely because of the quiet modesty of his manner from which the arrogance he might justifiably have assumed—and which is sometimes assumed by lesser men and drivers —was completely lacking. While he was dubbed with innumerable flamboyant pet names by the far from phlegmatic journalists of Italy, it is possible that his British friends' affectionate description as 'the great little man' was the more accurate. It seems to suit him better than: *figlio del diavolo; Mantovano volante; Nivola;* and even *il Maestro.*

Tazio Giorgio Nuvolari would have been the first to affirm that his father played an important part in his make-up, gave him the right to deserve well in the future. When he was only a little boy a farm horse kicked him right across the farmyard at Casteldario with shattering effects on his confidence. A few days later his father flung a gold coin under the horse's belly with the comment: 'If you want it, get it'. Fifty-five years later *il Maestro* still remembered this incident and often said that it was from that day he ceased to be afraid for himself and of fear itself.

It is but natural that a man of such outstanding skill, courage and grace, whose career on two and four wheels spanned over thirty years, should be surrounded by legend. As long ago as 1925, when none of the present-day champions were born, Tazio was badly hurt in an accident while testing a P2 Alfa Romeo at Monza. Typically, his first thoughts on being told that he would be confined to hospital for thirty days were that he would not take orders from mere doctors and secondly that he was due to ride for Bianchi in the Italian Grand Prix for motor cycles within ten days. Exerting all his personality he persuaded the hospital to encase him in plaster of Paris, and better still in the correct posture for lying on the tank. He was carried, accompanied by derisive laughter to the line and proceeded to lead from start to finish, covering the 190 miles at 75 m.p.h. Like some other drivers Nuvolari did not always take kindly to team discipline, largely because he was not convinced that all the team managers he met knew better than himself. Admittedly much of the so-called rivalry between the little man and Varzi—at least when they were both in the Alfa Romeo team—was nothing more than two combative men trying to argue their team manager into a sensible attitude. One of the better of the 'light relief' incidents occurred during the Tourist Trophy in Ulster when the Alfa team consisted of Campari, Nuvolari and Varzi. The practice days were enlivened by passionate argument as to the proposed finishing order, with the harassed manager performing a carefully rehearsed draw with matches of unequal length. Unfortunately for everyone a helpful Pressman got the story into the Italian newspapers, and the humourless

Mussolini was not amused. Cables rushed through informing all and sundry at Newtownards that the glory of Italy was more important than the pride of individual drivers; discipline must be maintained. So it was agreed that the finishing order would be Campari, Varzi, Nuvolari—unless it rained, in which case Nuvolari was to go through. Because of his preoccupation in appealing to the saints for rain Nuvolari made a very bad start, but soon the three Alfas were running in formation and everything looked set for a nice regular victory, until towards the end of the race when, to his delight, the Mantuan felt 'rain' on his face. Now he was in his element and his race started; down went his riding mechanic on the floor and the little aero screen was flattened. Engine speed went to the maximum and inches were saved everywhere as Tazio thrust on to victory. At the subsequent vociferous post-mortem the little man's innocent defence that it had been raining—his face and gaily patterned Fair Isle pullover were still wet—was spoilt when it was discovered that the radiator cap had been leaking.

While he was the fieriest of Italians, no sufferer of fools and could with provocation indicate precisely what he thought of those who impeded him during a race, he was among the most helpful of the master drivers to those interested in the technique of driving; no matter whether they were coming men or just students. Even driving the mildest of Italian saloons, or his little 4CV Renault, he had an uncanny knack of simulating racing conditions and demonstrating on the roads around his home town, Mantua, how one should drive a Grand Prix car at three times the speed. His demonstrations of the drift and how to use bumps to steer the car were unforgettable experiences. Like all great men he had a big heart and never allowed the chicanery and pettiness of those who inevitably surround the great to sully him; he kept aloof by insisting that he was a simple racing driver, not a politician, nor a model for advertisements, nor a business man. Apocryphal, or not, the story is told that after winning the Vanderbilt Cup on the Roosevelt Raceway in America a tooth-paste manufacturer approached him with bags of gold. He was rebuffed with the stinging comment that he was a racing driver and it gave him a modest living, he was not a model girl and had they seen his long horse-like teeth!

The affection and generosity with which he treated his friends, especially the youngsters among them, was only equalled by the affection in which he was held. The famous Dr. Ferdinand Porsche, at an official pre-war German reception when Caracciola, Rosemeyer and von Brauchitsch—as well as nationalistic representatives of the Nazi Party—were among the guests, described Nuvolari as the greatest ace of the past, the present and the future. Bold words but to some people no longer so young, true words.

It was probably the gentle modesty of Tazio's manner which attracted the mass of spectators to him rather than his exultant driving, and it was because of the sympathy forged between them and the fierce little man out on the circuit that he was chosen favourite of the crowds in Britain, France, Germany and Italy. Although completely lacking in arrogance, he knew he was the greatest driver in the world; not necessarily the most successful, but the greatest. Perhaps the repeatedly quoted story of three master drivers is the perfect illustration that others understood and appreciated his attitude: 'Caracciola says he is,

Rosemeyer obviously thinks he is, but, by now, Nuvolari knows he is the greatest driver'.

The common people, far away from the excitement of the racing scene, appreciated fully the unusual qualities of Nuvolari and repeatedly evidenced it by the respect, if not adulation, with which he was treated everywhere. Through the packed square of Brescia during scrutineering for the Mille Miglia, in the crowded market-place of his home town, Mantua, or anywhere in Italy, the crowd parted, the noise and argument of the crowd was stilled, the haggling around the stalls was hushed and one can think of few people less than the Pope for whom the excitements of everyday life would be easily forgotten. Any member of a royal family who received such steadfast loyalty and respect could indeed have felt secure on their throne. Such was the magnetism of the little man's personality (and in a latter era this was so true of Mike Hawthorn as well) that if he walked into a crowded room where not a soul knew him by sight, everyone would say 'Who's that?'

There are cynics, and unfortunately some of them have been racing drivers, who find it difficult to understand the force behind the masters in any profession or calling, except to comment in a vulgar fashion on their fantastic earnings. The earnings of Nuvolari, like those of Leonardo da Vinci, are no doubt recorded in the archives of some bank, but they are—and were to him—unimportant. What is important was his skill, courage and grace—the notes in bank files are not his life story; that was written indelibly on the circuits of the world. I hope I will

The moods—and 'uniforms'—of the man

not be considered immodest if I quote something I wrote elsewhere, as I find it difficult to put it differently. 'There is no doubt that the subconscious hope behind all outstanding effort, whether it be the conquering of Everest, the discovery of a previously unknown continent, or victory against almost insurmountable odds in a Grand Prix —as when *il Maestro* won the German Grand Prix in 1935—is to defeat oneself and not just the opposition. When Robert Falcon Scott lay down in his shuddering tent for the last time he knew he had defeated Scott and not just the Arctic wastes; when Hillary and Tensing came down through the South Cwm it was not the terror of the Himalayas they had beaten, but themselves; just as when Nuvolari achieved his greatest victories they were not victories over Caracciola, Rosemeyer or Varzi, but victories over himself—and the frightening horse away back in the farmyard at Casteldario. Tazio never developed the slightly theatrical approach of some: that he must appear and do well for the sake of his public. His appearances—particularly late in his life—and the combativeness of his driving were food and drink to him and a means of proving to himself that there was nothing of which he was not capable'.

As with Paganini, that other great Italian whom so many people believed had a pact with the devil, there were those—and among them was probably listed Varzi on occasion—who felt that Nuvolari's skill was more than natural. During the Mille Miglia of 1930 (which, unlike later versions of that race, finished in darkness) Varzi was comfortably settled in the lead and none of his glances in the mirror, nor those of his anxious backward-looking mechanic, revealed any traces of the headlamps of his rival Nuvolari. For miles Tazio had been driving without lights, so that the more powerful car driven by the relaxing Varzi could be caught without warning.

From Bologna on to Peschiera and Brescia—the reverse of the race direction later—Nuvolari with his riding mechanic Guidotti, now development engineer at Alfa Romeo, gained metre by metre. Finally only about 30 miles from the chequered flag, and after the battle had been waged for 970 miles, Tazio hurled his car past Varzi to snatch victory. It may, or may not, be true that one needs a pact with the devil to take such risks, it must be just as true that considerable cold-blooded intelligence was essential to think of such a stratagem in the heat of battle in that most emotional of all races.

Short memory tends to make one think that all innovations have happened fairly recently, but this is far from true. It was Tazio who initiated the saw-tooth method of cornering as an improvement on the classic line of the early twenties; it was he who discovered first the four-wheel drift; it was he who proved that the vaunted and single-minded discipline of the German teams could be beaten; and, perhaps most important, it was he who demonstrated thoroughly that a great heart can counteract a deficiency in horse power.

People who never saw Nuvolari and who, perhaps, tend to judge only by material success—which is no criterion of ability—probably find it impossible to understand fully the Nuvolari legend. Such are liable to ask how he would compare with present-day drivers. To answer is impossible, but, with the exception of Fangio, there is no driver to compare with him for the manner in which he combined so many talents. He was probably the last link between the heroic days of the past and the circus-like atmosphere of today. With the courage and

On Alfa Romeos. Monaco, 1933 . . .

. . . Montlhéry, 1935 . . .

. . . and practising at Monaco, 1936

E

Bugatti, Montlhéry, 1934

Auto Union, Donington, 1938

Maserati, Marseilles, 1946

determination of the pioneer drivers in the Paris–Madrid era, he equalled the moderns in his skill, artistry and intelligence. After his list of successes have become lost and confused, and even his flamboyant pet names forgotten, he will be remembered—perhaps the British understood him best—as the Great Little Man.

In his later years, particularly after his frenzied Mille Miglia drive in a little Cisitalia in 1947, Italian journalists repeatedly asked Nuvolari why he did not give up his dangerous profession. The little man's response was typical—he asked one of them if he expected to die in bed. The journalist replied 'Yes, naturally'. Nuvolari wound up the conversation by telling the journalist how much he admired his courage in going to bed every night: 'You expect to die in bed. I expect to die on the race track, so bed and motor racing are equally dangerous'.

Ironically, illness dragged him down and he died in bed, on August 11, 1953. A little earlier he expressed a last wish: 'Bury me in my uniform'.

He was laid out in his study, with the badge of the British Racing Drivers' Club and the bronze mask of himself presented to him by his friends in that Club on the wall above him.

To all visitors, Tazio Nuvolari appeared as if in a deep sleep, his strong brown face serene, his brow devoid of furrows. He was dressed in his yellow jersey with the mongram and tortoise, his blue helmet and trousers. In his hands was a crucifix.

The principal racing successes of **TAZIO NUVOLARI**

1922	2nd:	Circuit of Garda.
1924	1st:	Circuit of Tigullio; Circuit of Savio; Circuit of Polesine.
1927	1st:	Circuit of Garda; Rome G.P.
	2nd:	Coppa Ciano.
1928	1st:	Circuit of Alessandria; Circuit of Pozzo; Tripoli G.P.; Circuit of Messina; Montenero Cup.
	2nd:	Circuit of Cremona; Coppa Ciano.
	3rd:	Italian G.P.
1929	2nd:	Coppa Ciano; Monza G.P.
	3rd:	Tripoli G.P.
1930	1st:	Mille Miglia; Tourist Trophy; Coppa Ciano.
	3rd:	Masaryk G.P.
1931	1st:	Italian G.P.; Targa Florio; Coppa Ciano; Circuit of Three Provinces, Bologna.
	2nd:	Belgian G.P.
	3rd:	Coppa Acerbo.
1932	1st:	French G.P.; Italian G.P.; Monaco G.P.; Coppa Acerbo; Coppa Ciano; Coppa Principe di Piemonte; Targa Florio.
	2nd:	German G.P.; Marseilles G.P.
	3rd:	Monza G.P.
1933	1st:	Belgian G.P.; Le Mans 24-hour Race; Mille Miglia; Eifelrennen; Coppa Ciano; Nice

		G.P.; Nimes G.P.; Circuit of Alessandria; Tunis G.P.; Tourist Trophy.
	2nd:	Italian G.P.; Coppa Acerbo; Tripoli G.P.
	3rd:	Avusrennen; Masaryk G.P.
1934	1st:	Modena G.P.; Naples G.P.
	2nd:	Mille Miglia; Coppa Acerbo.
	3rd:	Masaryk G.P.; Coppa Ciano; Spanish G.P.
1935	1st:	German G.P.; Coppa Ciano; Nice G.P.; Pau G.P.; Circuit of Biella; Circuit of Bergamo; Valentino G.P.
	2nd:	Italian G.P.; Masaryk G.P.
	3rd:	Penya Rhin G.P.
1936	1st:	Hungarian G.P.; Coppa Ciano; Modena G.P.; Circuit of Milan; Penya Rhin G.P.; G. Vanderbilt Cup.
	2nd:	Italian G.P.; Eifelrennen.
1937	1st:	Circuit of Milan.
1938	1st:	Italian G.P.; Donington G.P.
1939	1st:	Yugoslav G.P.
	2nd:	Eifelrennen.
1946	1st:	Albi G.P.
	2nd:	Circuit of Mantua.
1947	1st:	Circuit of Parma.
	2nd:	Mille Miglia.
	3rd:	Lido Cup, Venice.

SIR HENRY BIRKIN

by RODNEY WALKERLEY

LIKE Tazio Nuvolari, the racing driver who became a legend, he was small, he was shy and not very approachable and he had a stammer. But he gave the impression of great physical strength and stamina. He wore white trousers, a blue open-necked jersey with a B.R.D.C. badge on the breast-pocket and, always, around his neck a blue and white polka-dot scarf knotted at the back to allow the ends to stream behind.

One thinks of him thus before the start of a memorable match race at Brooklands in 1932 when Tim Birkin, otherwise Sir Henry Birkin, Baronet, was at his tigerish best. He pulled on his close-fitting helmet, not a crash helmet, then his racing gloves and, sleeves rolled up, climbed up into the seat of the monster 4½-litre supercharged single-seater Bentley. A few minutes later he was swooping high on the Brooklands bankings in pursuit of burly John Cobb in the aluminium-bodied 10½-litre Delage, a few lengths ahead after a better take-off. The match was for three laps between the two fastest cars then seen at the Wey-bridge track, built in 1906 as the world's first banked racing course when 100 m.p.h. was a very fast pace; that day the two cars were averaging well over 130 m.p.h. From start to finish Birkin never lifted his foot, the great car shooting through the air with all four wheels off the track when he hit the notorious bump on the river bridge. On the last lap, sportsman John Cobb held his car as low on the banking as he could. Birkin moved higher, closed, roared past and won by perhaps a length with a new lap record at 137·3 m.p.h.

Tim Birkin, who was never known by any other name, was one of the colourful personalities of the motoring world of the thirties, a type that seems to have vanished into history with their cars and their victories and their laurels. He took over, in the public eye, the film-star glamour that had surrounded Sir Henry Segrave a few years earlier.

Birkin started racing at Brooklands in 1921 with a French D.F.P., the little 2-litre car that W. O. Bentley had raced in the Tourist Trophy of 1914 before he began building the famous cars, with which Birkin himself was to find fame. Then for six years he stayed out of racing to establish himself a business, returning in 1928 to finish third, with a 3-litre Bentley, in the Essex Six Hours at Brooklands.

There were, at that time, no professional or 'works' teams in this country. There were wealthy men, titled men and many who raced were engaged in the motor trade, like Malcolm Campbell. Birkin, like the amateurs, raced for love of the finest of all sports, even if the prestige that rapidly surrounded his name did no harm to the motor business he had set up with Mike Couper, himself a Brooklands driver.

Birkin's first big victory came in 1929. He was then a member of the 'Bentley Boys' Le Mans team of works cars, most of them amateurs and friends of millionaire, Woolf Barnato, men like Jack Dunfee, theatrical agent and impresario, Sammy Davis, journalist, Dr. Benjafield, a

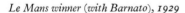

Le Mans winner (with Barnato), 1929

. . . 'swooping high on the Brooklands bankings' (1930)

Harley Street bacteriologist, all of whom brought a gaiety to their racing, which, to the astonishment of the foreign drivers, never interfered with the competence of their driving in the great Twenty-four Hour Race at Le Mans. That year, 1929, Birkin partnered Barnato in the winning speed six Bentley, at the then resounding average speed of 73·6 m.p.h., and the fourth of the five further victories for the marque.

Birkin was not by nature a team driver and was unhappy under rigid team control. In 1930 his own Bentleys, including the 4½-litre supercharged single-seat Brooklands car, were bought and sponsored by the Hon. Dorothy Paget, a woman who raced horses and was regarded by some of us as mildly eccentric. She maintained the cars for that season and then returned to the Turf.

That year Mercedes arrived at Le Mans with a 7-litre supercharged SS Mercedes to be driven by Caracciola and Werner. Birkin was there with his private team and again Barnato, chairman of Bentleys, headed the factory team. Before the race, W. O. Bentley and Birkin agreed to race their cars as one team against the Mercedes and Birkin was in his element as the man who was to drive on the limit to harry Caracciola into using his supercharger (which could be engaged and disengaged) for hours on end and thus wreck his engine. The race is history. Birkin and Caracciola duelled, passing and repassing, from the drop of the starting flag. Three of the five Bentleys failed to survive, including Birkin's, but the Mercedes duly broke down during the night with flat battery and flickering oil gauge, and the two 6½-litre Bentleys finished first and second, winning the Index of Performance handicap as well.

The duel was repeated in Phoenix Park, Dublin, a month later, in torrential rain, when, as Birkin remarked, Caracciola had no equal. The Mercedes was giving the Bentley a handicap start of two laps, and the German drove at tremendous speed, breaking the lap record time and time again in his efforts to shake off Birkin and wear down the handicap; for once Caracciola skidded as he braked and spun the big car in two great circles. Then the Bentley broke an oil pipe. The quick repair consumed his handicap and after a second unwanted stop Birkin dropped back to fifth place. 'I could not wish for a better race,' he wrote, 'nor a finer opponent. I thought in 1929 that he could never improve on his performance in the rain at Belfast [in the Tourist Trophy] but that day he proved me wrong'.

That September Birkin took his open four-seater Le Mans Bentley south to the French Grand Prix, held on a circuit outside Pau. His arrival with a sports car was greeted with derisive French laughter, but Birkin was unperturbed as he stood by the car that weighed all of two tons and towered above the surrounding Bugattis and Delage Grand Prix cars. But Birkin's plan was to use his 200 horsepower down the 6-mile straight and thus make up what he must lose in cornering.

It was perhaps his greatest race in a great career. With his dotted scarf streaming behind, he inexorably passed car after car on sheer speed, and held the Bentley on the limit through the curves. Towards the end of the 247-miles race, only Philippe Etancelin's Bugatti was in front and the Bentley was closing on that car. So, when the flag finally fell, Birkin thundered into second place and to a standing ovation from the crowd.

Except for his appearances at Brooklands with the single-seater, which once caught fire under him and forced him to jump from the cockpit as it slowed, Birkin's Bentley days were over. As there was

Le Mans, 1931

nothing in England, he had to look abroad for a road racing car. With Earl Howe as co-driver, he won again at Le Mans in 1931 and beat the great Giuseppe Campari's Alfa Romeo for first place in the Eireann cup at Dublin. With a Maserati he became the first Mountain Circuit Champion at Brooklands.

He disliked any form of handicap racing and fully approved when the Bentleys were withdrawn from a Tourist Trophy in Ulster, pointing out that the handicap was impossible on that Ards circuit where smaller cars had to be lapped time and time again on a course where passing was nothing but dangerous. As for Brooklands, he wrote: 'I think it is, without exception, the most out-of-date, inadequate and dangerous track in the world'. These words brought a libel action which was eventually settled out of court and a form of apology had to be inserted in every copy of his fine book *Full Throttle*.

In Brooklands racing he was required to break lap records at speeds never envisaged when the bankings were planned but he continued to give the crowds what they had paid to see and, in 1931, he won the Gold Star Handicap. It was typical of the man that, when he returned to the Paddock and was told that he had been disqualified, he shrugged and refused to make a protest. He admitted he had crossed his limit line on the unbanked curve past the Fork, where cars of varying speeds were allotted separate channels. He merely apologized, remarking with his stammer, that he was going so fast to beat his handicap that he could not hold the car to the set line. His single-seater Bentley circled the bankings at between 135 and 140 m.p.h., and he knew he was taking his life literally in his hands every time he flew through the air over the big bump on the bridge across the River Wey.

The year 1933 was a year of tragedies. In Berlin, Otto Merz was killed on the Avus, and the racing at Peronne, in Picardy, cost the lives of Guy Bouriat and Louis Trintignant, brother of France's latter day champion.

Grand Prix racing was the hunting ground of the Bugatti, the Maserati and the new P.3 Alfa Romeo. Birkin took his Maserati over to Tripoli, for the Grand Prix on the Mellaha circuit of Italy's new Lybian 'empire'. Achille Varzi won the race with a Bugatti, Nuvolari (Alfa Romeo) was second and Birkin was a close third. But during the race—he drove as usual with sleeves rolled above the elbow—his bare arm touched the exhaust pipe. In spite of medical attention, the burn turned septic. It is also said that he was, at the time, in pain from his appendix, but had postponed the operation in order to race. His old racing companion, Dr. J. D. Benjafield, fought for his life in London, but three weeks later Tim Birkin was dead, his brilliant career cut short.

The principal racing successes of **SIR HENRY BIRKIN**

1928	3rd:	Essex Six Hours, Brooklands.
1929	1st:	Le Mans 24-hour Race.
	3rd:	Spa 24-hour Race.
1930	2nd:	French G.P.
1931	1st:	Le Mans 24-hour Race; Brooklands Mountain Championship.
	2nd:	Irish G.P.
1932	3rd:	Belgian Touring Car G.P.
1933	3rd:	Tripoli G.P.

RUDOLF CARACCIOLA

by RICHARD VON FRANKENBERG

Acknowledging the crowd after his first German G.P. victory (1926)...

...and the flag after his sixth (1939)

ABOARD the pleasure steamers on Lake Lugano, guides point out to inquiring visitors the beauty spots and noteworthy sights, the mountains, churches and famous villas. And as this steamer reaches Castagnola, suburb of Lugano, and turns towards the eastern point of the lake, they often say 'Down there, between the cypress-trees, you see the Villa Favorita which belongs to the famous industrialist Thyssen and houses one of the largest private art collections in the world.' And then they point upward to the suburb of Ruvigliano—'The villa you see next to the church up there, belonged to the German racing driver Rudolf Caracciola, who finally adopted Swiss nationality and died in 1959. He lies buried in the small cemetery up there.'

In many European countries, if one were to take a poll today, not necessarily among motoring enthusiasts but 'among the people' as it were, to find out which racing driver had been the most popular, whose name had become a household word, one would find that of Caracciola high on the list. At the very least, his name would be spoken in the same breath as those of Fangio and Moss. Among the German sportsmen of the past who are still universally remembered, Caracciola—'Carratsch'—is bracketed with Max Schmelling, the boxer.

There are few sportsmen whose fame survives one generation, just as but a few actors and stars take with them more than the fame of their day. Even in the field of light athletics ten, twenty, thirty years hence, one will probably recall only the Finnish runner Nurmi, who reached his zenith in the twenties; perhaps Jesse Owens and Zatopek, but not many more; in Soccer, the fame of Stanley Matthews and the Brazilian Pele, will remain in the eye of the world—for a time.

And in motor sport? Here too there are only too few personalities—a statement which may hurt many enthusiasts, but we ought not to see our particular world as though it were the only one—and these were few men, who will be talked about tens of years hence, whom everyone knows: Nuvolari in Italy, Caracciola in Germany, Fangio in the Argentine and in England, Moss. These at least in my opinion are the only candidates for permanent places in the memories of tomorrow.

There were faster German drivers than Rudolf Caracciola. Bernd Rosemeyer, for example, could drive faster than Caracciola; Manfred von Brauchitsch, too, often put in faster laps and, during his best years from 1937 to 1939, Hermann Lang was a faster driver. Berghe von Trips, to give a more recent example, must, I think, also be placed above Caracciola, as far as pure speed is concerned.

But none of these attained success either as great or as often as did Caracciola. For fourteen years from 1926 to 1939 his name hit the headlines. He won, to list only a few of his most striking and important achievements, the first German Grand Prix (for sports cars) in 1926, the 1929 Tourist Trophy at Ards in Ireland and the 1931 Mille Miglia; he won the Swiss Grand Prix in 1935, 1937 and 1938, the Italian

Grand Prix in 1934 and 1937, the 1935 French and Belgian Grands Prix, the 1935 Tripoli G.P. and the 1936 Monaco G.P. On the Nürburgring he won the German Grand Prix five times. He won everywhere, and in 1938 on the day when Rosemeyer lost his life trying to surpass his best-ever performance, he drove a streamlined Mercedes-Benz over a mile along the Autobahn near Frankfurt, at a speed of 432·7 k.p.h., 266·88 m.p.h., the highest speed ever achieved on a road.

On examining the list of his successes, two things stand out: first, except for the 1932 season Caracciola has always driven for Daimler-Benz; Caracciola and Mercedes became in time synonymous. Few other drivers have remained quite so loyal and when he joined Alfa in 1932, it was by express permission of Daimler-Benz, for the Untertürkheim firm did not intend to race in 1932 or 1933 and welcomed the opportunity for their top driver to keep in form by driving an Alfa.

After the War, too, Caracciola drove for Daimler-Benz on three occasions. Even after the end of his career in 1952, at Monza in 1954 for example, he could still occasionally be seen in the stands among the spectators when a Mercedes team was racing. He was a living advertisement for his firm, and Daimler-Benz owe a great many of their victories in famous races all over the world to his talent.

The second remarkable point in any analysis of his successes is the fact that the number of his victories is quite out of proportion with his lap records. In other words: it was usually another who drove the fastest lap, but the winner, at the count in the end, was Caracciola . . .

This, I believe, is the secret of his sustained success—moderation, consistency and a sensitivity for the limits of mechanism. Certainly, during the great run of German racing successes of 1934 and 1939 a great deal was done by Daimler-Benz to secure for his car a place that would be tactically right and would become by the end of a race a first place. But Alfred Neubauer, who as racing manager was nearly as legendary a figure as was Caracciola as driver, did not pursue these pro-Caracciola tactics merely because he found Caracciola an agreeable fellow, but simply because he could rely on him as on nobody else.

Carratsch never overstrained the engines, Carratsch drove extremely evenly and spared his tyres—at the time of 500-km Grands Prix, this alone could be decisive. Moreover, Carratsch was seldom involved in accidents. In 1939 he slid out of races twice, but fairly harmlessly. During these years no other mishap comes to mind except one in 1933, which is discussed later.

At the Nürburgring before the war, 10 minutes represented the 'sound-barrier' as it were (only during the last few years has this been reduced to 9 minutes). But it does not appear to have been one of Caracciola's ambitions to lap the Ring in under 10 minutes; in fact he usually remained a few seconds or fractions of a second above this. In practice for the 1937 German Grand Prix for example, Rosemeyer put in the best time with an Auto Union, 9 minutes 46·2 seconds; Hermann Lang achieving 9 minutes 52·2 seconds and Manfred von Brauchitsch 9 minutes 55·2 seconds—while Caracciola contented himself with 10 minutes 0·40 seconds. But Caracciola won the race!

Whether he could have bettered 10 minutes at the Nürburgring, had he wished to do so (and ignoring all considerations of equipment) I cannot say. But that Caracciola was certainly not slow when speed was of importance he proved with his practice times at Berne in 1937, when he was concerned to get on to the front row of the grid. He drove

'Carratsch' tousled (Phoenix Park, Dublin 1930) . . .

. . . and dapper (Monaco 1937)

five fast laps, none of them substantially more than 2 minutes 34 seconds, one of them in 2 minutes 32 seconds; Rosemeyer who was placed second on the grid, achieved 2 minutes 33 seconds. That 2 minutes 32 seconds lap, which was never beaten before this wonderful course was closed in 1954 by an anxious local government voting against motor sport, is a time which must surely silence all critics.

Caracciola's driving was definitely 'soft', which is the reason for his developing into so excellent a driver in rain.

For me Caracciola's greatest race was the 1936 Grand Prix of Monaco. Rain poured down unceasingly, a fact reflected in the average speeds. Carratsch won at 51·69 m.p.h. (Fagioli had won the 1935 race in a lighter car at an average speed of 58·17 m.p.h.). Achille Varzi (Auto Union) finished almost 2 minutes behind Caracciola, and a lap behind Hans Stuck finished third.

I was then in my 'teens and although I attended races as a spectator, I was quite unable to judge driving performances. I did, however, have the opportunity retrospectively in 1959 when I drove a 1936–7 5·6-litre Grand Prix car on the Daimler-Benz test track. In comparison with the racing car of today, this supercharged monster, which in the end had a power unit developed to give 646 b.h.p. but weighed no more than 750 kg., was a car without reasonable road-holding or brakes. It could be steered only with the use of enormous physical strength, and even on a dry road, the rear wheels could be spun almost at will—juggling with the accelerator pedal could result simply in a game on one spot! Not until the day when I drove this car did I begin to appreciate the ability required to race such a car around the sinuous Monaco circuit. I took my hat off to the drivers of those days, and in particular to Rudolf Caracciola.

Rudolf Caracciola lived to the age of 58. He was born at Remagen on the Rhine, where his father owned an hotel, on January 30, 1901. To this day you can see painted in large letters on the front of the Hotel Fürstenberg: 'Formerly Caracciola'.

The name sounds Italian, and was pronounced in the Italian manner but the family had in fact lived in Germany for generations.

Caracciola's family would have liked to see their son Rudolf take over his father's hotel. But he didn't welcome the idea, and after his first experiences with engines when driving the hotel's motor boat about on the Rhine wanted instead to handle cars; his family consequently sent him to Fafnir at Aachen.

Since he was keenly interested in motor sport, and had meanwhile won the 'Round Cologne' reliability trial on his private NSU motor-cycle, Fafnir twice put a car at his disposal. With this Fafnir he took part in his first race on four wheels at Avus on June 1, 1922, and was placed fourth in his class; a month later he won the Opelbahn race at Rüsselheim in the same car. A year later Fafnir sent him to Dresden as their sales representative. There, in the spring of 1923, a friend lent him a small 4-h.p. Ego car (a make which existed from 1912 to 1925) for a track race at Berlin. Surprisingly he won that race for his class, beating a number of established drivers.

Some weeks later he applied for work at Daimler Motoren Unter-türkheim—he had come to know a Director of Daimlers at Dresden, and gone to Württemberg on his recommendations. The management gave the task of trying out the young Caracciola to their famous racing driver Christian Werner, who did so—on the roads around Stuttgart.

Except for his early races and a spell with Alfa (Monaco 1932) . . .

However, the 22-year-old Caracciola was not in consequence employed as racing driver. He became instead a salesman at their branch in Dresden, with a monthly salary of one hundred marks and a half per cent commission on every car sold. But within a few weeks he was given one of the new Mercedes Sports cars to use in various competitions.

With this 6/25/40 Mercedes (it was the first series of supercharged cars having a 1·5-litre engine), Caracciola won, on July 5, 1923, the Touring car category in the ADAC-Reichsfahrt, an important event, and shortly afterwards three hill-climbs. Attention thus began to focus on Caracciola, and 1924 saw him entered in a number of international hill-climbs. When he had won the Klausen event in Switzerland, as well as several in Germany and Czechoslovakia, he became officially a 'works driver'. Incidentally, the 6/24/40-h.p. supercharged Mercedes which he drove during this period had a top speed of only 124 k.p.h. (77 m.p.h.) when timed over the measured kilometre. He also took part in the Touring car race of 1925, but now in the large 6-litre super-charged car (24/100/140) and in the 1926 German Grand Prix began in earnest his great career in sports and racing cars.

Then he drove for Alfa Romeo in 1932, proving surprisingly fast in the dainty 2·3-litre Alfa Romeo P.3—a very different car to the heavy 35-cwt. SS Mercedes—and winning nine times. In 1933, however, Alfa Romeo withdrew from racing. It was then that Caracciola and Chiron, who had become firm friends, decided to found their own racing partnership with two ex-works Alfa Romeos. They intended to race first in the Monaco G.P. and there the short-lived partnership came to an end. On one of the last practice laps of the first session, a front wheel brake on Caracciola's car locked as he entered the chicane left-hander. The car skidded against a wall and Caracciola was seriously injured: the fracture of his right thigh was extremely complicated and as a permanent legacy one of his legs was shortened. For months he lay in plaster, for months he was treated by specialists, for months Charlotte

. . . always a Mercedes man: Tourist Trophy 1929 . . .

. . . French G.P., 1935 . . .

. . . Swiss G.P., 1937

Caracciola—Charly, his wife who followed him wherever he went—was filled with anxiety for him. When winter came, they both returned to Aroso, where Carratsch loved to ski. The mountain air was to complete his recovery. One evening, his wife did not return from a ski-tour: an avalanche had killed her.

This was a terrible year for Caracciola.

He was of course asked to return to Daimler-Benz at the beginning of the 1934 season, when their new Grand Prix car the W.25 for the 750 kg. Formula, was being tried out. His leg at least was sufficiently healed for him to work the pedals—but would he ever be fast again, as fast as before the long painful pause, who could say? Daimler-Benz certainly couldn't and this was one of the reasons why they engaged another ace driver, the Italian Luigi Fagioli.

Events showed, however, that Caracciola quickly returned to his old form. He was after all still young, only 33 years of age. He remained the most successful Mercedes driver, remained the great Caracciola, until 1939 and the outbreak of the Second World War.

At the time of his accident at Monte Carlo, he had been living in Switzerland and he married again in 1937 to Alice Caracciola, who had tasted motor sport from the stands during her first marriage and knew many of the racing drivers. She became his ideal partner and still lives in the Caracciola villa at Ruvigliana near Lugano. Today, no one possesses more complete archives covering lap-times and positions of all pre-war races.

Carratsch could not have wished for a better partner, when he had his second serious accident, shortly after the war. By then a Swiss citizen, he was invited to race at Indianapolis in 1946. During training he had a terrible accident when something struck his head—a bird or perhaps a stone? who knows? Some even ascribed the accident to an act of sabotage although I find this difficult to believe. He lay unconscious for eleven days and years passed before he overcame this accident. But at the age of 51, when Daimler-Benz re-entered motor sport, he too tried to make a come-back. First of all he took part in the Monte Carlo Rally in a Mercedes, and succeeded in finishing a few places ahead of his Mercedes colleagues Hermann Lang and Karl Kling.

Looking back on this come-back in perspective, it must be considered foolish. The idea was of course born of the entirely valid feeling that racing was his whole life, and who gives up gladly the one thing that means more to him than anything else in the world? But in great racing, there is no place among the top drivers for a 51-year-old man who is making a return after an interval of twelve years and serious concussion.

Be that as it may, Caracciola entered for the 1952 Mille Miglia in the 'gull-wing' 300 SL and, remarkably, finished fourth in the general classification. His Mercedes colleague Karl Kling, however, finished well ahead of him, second overall, and Fagioli, with whom he had once driven in the same Mercedes G.P. team, managed to finish third in a far slower 2-litre Lancia.

Then Caracciola took up the fight again in a sports car race at the Bremgarten circuit; a fight which ended against an enormous tree where his car had been hurled after it had been thrown from the track. Once again he lay in hospital with complicated thigh fractures. And that of course was the end of his career.

Last competitive appearance. Practising at Berne, 1952

But no one ever held against Caracciola the fact that he tried this come-back, nor that he failed in it. He has remained the legendary figure of pre-1939 days, the years of his great achievements.

He died at Kassel seven years after his last race. One of his old friends, world motor-cycle record-holder Ernst Henne, went to him at the Clinic where he lay, where even the best doctors could do little for him: Caracciola was suffering from a liver complaint, at an acute stage and incurable.

For the passengers aboard the pleasure steamer on lake Lugano, there remains only a fleeting memory of the villa up there, the famous name . . . one soon forgets, turning to other attractions. But in the world of sport, this Rudolf Caracciola remains one of the few who will never be forgotten.

The principal racing successes of **RUDOLF CARACCIOLA**

1926	1st:	German G.P.
1927	1st:	Eifelrennen.
1928	1st:	German G.P.
1929	1st:	Tourist Trophy.
	3rd:	Monaco G.P.
1930	1st:	Eireann Cup; Irish G.P.
1931	1st:	German G.P.; Mille Miglia; Avusrennen; Eifelrennen.
1932	1st:	German G.P.; Monza G.P.; Eifelrennen; Lwow G.P.
	2nd:	Monaco G.P.; Avusrennen; Coppa Acerbo.
	3rd:	French G.P.
1934	2nd:	Spanish G.P.

1935	1st:	Belgian G.P.; French G.P.; Spanish G.P.; Eilferennen; Tripoli G.P.
	2nd:	Swiss G.P.; Penya Rhin G.P.
	3rd:	German G.P.
1936	1st:	Monaco G.P.; Tunis G.P.
	2nd:	Penya Rhin G.P.
1937	1st:	German G.P.; Italian G.P.; Swiss G.P.; Masaryk G.P.
	2nd:	Monaco G.P.; Eifelrennen.
	3rd:	Donington G.P.
1938	1st:	Swiss G.P.; Coppa Acerbo.
	2nd:	French G.P.; German G.P.; Pau G.P.
	3rd:	Italian G.P.
1939	1st:	German G.P.
	2nd:	Swiss G.P.
	3rd:	Eifelrennen.

His pre-war approach to racing was serious, even ruthless (1930)...

ACHILLE VARZI

by GIANNI MARIN

DURING the late twenties and early thirties a double transformation took place in motor sport. The first change occurred as the cars of the immediate post-war period were superseded by the much more modern and technically very different cars of which the famous Fiat 804 and Alfa Romeo P.2 were the forerunners. The second, just as fundamental, was that driving technique was brought up to date by the demands of these new Grand Prix machines.

In this period Achille Varzi and Tazio Nuvolari worthily upheld the great Italian driving tradition and became the heirs of the great masters of the original style—Nazzaro, Bordino, Antonio Ascari, Salamano, Giaccone . . .

At that time, a great fighting driver, Emilio Materassi, dominated Italian racing. Also in the field were Brilli Peri, Campari, Alfieri Maserati, who, however, had already gone into manufacturing, Enzo Ferrari, who was not yet running the stable by which he was to become most famous, and other drivers of lesser stature such as Aimo Maggi, Bogna and Pugno, most of whom were pure amateurs.

Together with Nuvolari and Taruffi, Varzi entered the racing car lists from motor cycling. When Varzi and Nuvolari raced against each other on four wheels for the first time at Verona, on a wet, windy day in 1927, Nuvolari won. On the old circuit at Alessandria came a 'return match'. Bordino lost his life during practice when he hit a dog and crashed. Nuvolari was first again, and the race showed Varzi to be the antithesis of the Mantuan. One was unrestrained impetus, the other order and style. At the start Varzi changed a sparking plug, chased hard, put in the fastest lap and at the finish was on Nuvolari's tail. Two new champions had been born, each as different as the two sides of a coin, but to be bound together throughout their careers by an intimate rivalry. Then the season followed its course and Materassi won the Targa Florio, then the Perugia Cup Race; in the Rome G.P. it was Nuvolari's turn to win, while at Bologna, where Varzi did not compete because he had no car, Materassi was again the winner.

Varzi's fulfilment came when he decided to race on his own and to buy the car he was to drive to his first great successes—a P.2 Alfa Romeo which he took over from Campari on the eve of the European Grand Prix at Monza. Chiron won that race in a Bugatti, but in his five-year-old car Varzi was second and showed out of the ordinary senses of tactics, endurance, shrewdness and style. At the time Varzi was 24 years old—he was born on August 8, 1904 at Galliate in the province of Novara—and was quite uncharacteristically blond for a Latin and as slim as a greyhound.

In 1929 he drove for Alfa Romeo: third in the Mille Miglia, first in the Rome G.P., at Alessandria, in the Trieste–Opicina event, at Montenero Circuit and in the Monza Grand Prix, where after a late pit stop he had to make up two minutes in the last 60 miles.

. . . but he mellowed for his post-war come-back (1947)

F

Although too much has sometimes been made of the personal rivalry between Nuvolari and Varzi, there was really no room for both of them in the 1930 Alfa Romeo team, so after gaining a place for them in the Mille Miglia and a first at Alessandria he ran against them in the Targa Florio in his old P.2—and won. But increasingly he drove a Maserati, winning the San Sebastian Grand Prix, the Coppa Acerbo and the Monza Grand Prix. In that year, for the second time, his successes gained him the title Champion of Italy.

For three years, from 1931 to 1933, he raced as a member of the Bugatti team. Although their cars were sometimes outclassed, in 1931 Varzi won the Tunis Grand Prix, the Pietro Bordino circuit, in the Susa-Mon Cenisio event and, with Chiron, the French Grand Prix. In 1932 he completely dominated the Tunis Grand Prix and was classified first in the 3-litre class of the Rome Royal Prix; fourth overall at Montenero, second at Schauinsland and absolute fifth in the Monza Grand Prix. In 1933 he won the Monaco Grand Prix for Bugatti after a wheel-to-wheel duel with Nuvolari, the Tripoli Grand Prix and, with a 4·9-litre Bugatti, the Avusrennen and he was placed second in the Susa-Mon Cenisio event and in the Belgian Grand Prix; he was fourth in the Coppa Acerbo and in the Spanish Grand Prix.

When Alfa Romeo withdrew from racing Varzi joined Ferrari and thus once again drove Alfas. The season started unfavourably—in the Monaco Grand Prix he had to be content with sixth place—but he soon got back into style by being first in the Mille Miglia, in the Pietro Bordino Circuit (Alessandria), the Coppa Ciano, the Tripoli Grand Prix, the Targa Florio, the Penya Rhin Grand Prix and the Nice Grand Prix. He also gained a string of seconds and thirds and at the end of the season was once again declared Champion of Italy.

He drove for the Auto Union in the two following seasons but, although he had less difficulty than most in adapting himself to the rear-engined cars, did not gather the hoped-for laurels. However, in 1935, he won the Tunis G.P. and the Coppa Acerbo, was second in the

During his greatest duel with Nuvolari (Monaco, 1933)

Tripoli G.P., third in the Avusrennen. 1936 brought him a second at Monaco, thirds in the Hungarian Grand Prix and in the Coppa Acerbo and a fourth in the Swiss Grand Prix.

He won at San Remo with a Maserati in 1937 and was then sixth in the Italian Grand Prix with an Auto Union. But his health was declining, especially on account of drugs supplied to him by so-called friends. He became a patient in a nursing-home, and not until after the Second World War was he able to return to racing.

This was 1946 when he was once again received with open arms by Alfa Romeo. The new Varzi drove the Type 158 with his old assurance and once again won a Grand Prix at Turin and finished second to Trossi at Milan. In 1947 he went to South America, finishing second in the Buenos Aires Grand Prix, first at Rosario and Interlagos. Back in Europe he finished second in three *grandes épreuvres*, the Swiss, European (Belgian) and Italian Grands Prix and also won the Bari Grand Prix.

And so we come to 1948. He went to South America again and drove an Alfa Romeo into second place in the Mar del Plata Grand Prix and then went on to win for the second time the Interlagos Grand Prix. In the Bari Grand Prix for the Coppa Brasile, he raced with Cisitalia and was placed third; he had the same result with the same type of car at Mantua.

Then to the Bremgarten circuit and tragedy. It was June 30, 1948, and that Berne meeting was doubly tragic for as well as Varzi it robbed motor sport of Christian Kautz and a great motor cycling champion, Omobono Tenni.

Before this fatal moment, Varzi had had only one serious racing accident, at Tunis in 1936 when the rear suspension of his Auto Union failed; he left the road at about 125 m.p.h. and by a miracle was not even scratched. Thirteen years had to elapse—with so many risks in so many events—before fate had to betray Varzi when he of all men, should have been safe. Probably he was trying to improve his times when, in practice in rain and on a greasy wet road, he entered a left-hander at around 110 m.p.h.; Varzi lost the tail of the Alfa and the skid which developed to a broadside had to lengthen out for just so many metres before the driver could begin to straighten it into a half-turn, during this half-turn the tail of the car had to bump a pole (the only one on a slight slope flanking the road), by this time most of the speed had been dissipated but the car had to be swung by this impact against a bank where it overturned, killing instantly the driver who had remained in his driving seat. It had to happen, it was marked in the book of fate.

Nobody who knew Achille Varzi could have thought that he would have an accident like this or that he would lose his life on a race circuit. It might have been said that he was without nerves, for his calmness seemed to demonstrate this on many varied occasions.

Achille Varzi was a stylist who tended to instinctively make an art of the profession. The secret of this very peculiar ability Varzi himself could perhaps have not described—it seemed to stem from an extraordinary knack of being able to assess for any given set of conditions at any point on any circuit the limits of road-holding. He was also scrupulous—sometimes pedantic—in the general and detailed preparation of himself and his car. Before every race Achille Varzi left nothing to chance in a slow methodic work of care, thought and examination

With Alfa Romeos. Contemplative at Montlhéry, 1934 . . .

. . . concentrating at Berne, 1947

which neglected nothing: the condition of his own car, the road to be raced over, his opponents' cars, the outlook and preferences of the drivers to be faced. Over the years experience amalgamated all this subtle, penetrating, intelligent mental work and it was nearly always with anticipatory vision of what the events and developments of the race should 'logically' be that Varzi started. He was rarely wrong and he has left memorable examples—for example at Interlagos in Brazil in 1947, when it was really before the start that Varzi won by reasoning a race which seemed desperate.

Other drivers may have inspired more enthusiasm than Varzi on account of their dash, others may have given crowds more passing thrills but few have shown more convincing 'class'. During a race his consistency was exemplary and this in cars which seldom lent themselves to smooth continuity, as do those of today.

Varzi had no preference for a particular type of circuit. He was a master alike of tortuous circuits and high-speed autodromes. He excelled at Monza, but he had won the Targa Florio; he excelled at Tripoli, but had won at Monte Carlo. A master everywhere. And everywhere he showed that marvellous style of his, clean and smooth; at the same time he was a very sensitive man, deeply enamoured of the sport of motor racing.

The principal racing successes of **ACHILLE VARZI**

1928	2nd:	Italian G.P.; Circuit of Alessandria.
	3rd:	Tripoli G.P.
1929	1st:	Coppa Ciano; Monza G.P.; Rome G.P.; Circuit of Alessandria.
	2nd:	Spanish Touring Car G.P.
	3rd:	Mille Miglia; Circuit of Cremona; Messina Cup.
1930	1st:	Targa Florio; Coppa Acerbo; Monza G.P.; Circuit of Alessandria; Spanish G.P.
	2nd:	Mille Miglia.
	3rd:	Tourist Trophy.
1931	1st:	Circuit of Alessandria; Tunis G.P.
	3rd:	German G.P.; Monaco G.P.; Monza G.P.; Targa Florio.
1932	1st:	Tunis G.P.
	3rd:	Targa Florio.
1933	1st:	Monaco G.P.; Avusrennen; Tripoli G.P.
	2nd:	Belgian G.P.

1934	1st:	Mille Miglia; Targa Florio; Coppa Ciano; Circuit of Alessandria; Penya Rhin G.P.; Tripoli G.P.; Nice G.P.
	2nd:	French G.P.; Avusrennen; Circuit of Biella; Modena G.P.
	3rd:	Montreux G.P.
1935	1st:	Coppa Acerbo; Tunis G.P.
	2nd:	Tripoli G.P.
	3rd:	Avusrennen.
1936	1st:	Tripoli G.P.
	2nd:	Monaco G.P.; Circuit of Milan; Swiss G.P.
	3rd:	Hungarian G.P.; Coppa Acerbo.
1937	1st:	San Remo G.P.
1946	1st:	Valentino G.P.
	2nd:	Milan G.P.
1947	1st:	Bari G.P.; Rosario G.P.
	2nd:	Belgian G.P.; Italian G.P.; Swiss G.P.
1948	2nd:	Mar del Plata G.P.
	3rd:	Bari G.P.; Circuit of Mantua.

1932

LOUIS CHIRON

by W. F. BRADLEY

LOUIS ALEXANDRE CHIRON has behind him the enviable reputation of twenty-eight years as a professional racing driver, and a career during which he competed in more than 250 events of various types.

Chiron has the distinction of possessing dual nationality. Born in the Principality of Monaco in August 1899, he was naturally entitled to a Monégasque passport. But his father was a French citizen, which gave the boy the right to claim acceptance as a Frenchman. To prove that this was no idle gesture, he volunteered for military service during the First World War, and was sent to the front as an artilleryman before he was eighteen years of age (and was later chauffeur to Marshals Foch and Petain).

When only 13 years of age he had passed the French driving test which gave him the right to take a car on the road. During the early post-war period the ambition of many a full-blooded youth was to get possession of a Bugatti. Chiron succeeded in 1923 when he became the proud owner of a 1500 c.c. Bugatti and took part, in a purely amateur capacity, in a number of hill-climbs organized by the Moto Club de Nice. He made his début as a professional, or at least a semi-professional, in 1924 when he took part in six events, most of them hill-climbs, finishing second, third and fourth and, at the end of the year, securing a first with a 2-litre Bugatti.

The year 1925 was a busy one, when in addition to local hill-climbs and short-distance speed contests, he took part in open races at Monza, Comminges, and the Grand Prix de la Côte d'Azur. In this latter event he finished second behind Robert Benoist (who was driving a much bigger Delage) thus founding an international reputation and securing for him a position on the Bugatti works team.

Chiron has all the characteristics of a Meridional: quick in action, vivacious, restless, somewhat inclined to impatience with the slower-moving Northerners. It is thus hardly surprising that the races he looks back upon with the greatest pleasure are those which brought him in close contact with his competitors. He has a particular liking for Nürburgring, not merely on account of its natural difficulties, but because there he was always at close grips with fellow drivers; Spa interested him too and naturally the Monaco races stand high in his estimation.

To the general public, Chiron and Bugatti were for years most often associated with the Targa Florio. Chiron, however, describes this race as a somewhat overrated long-drawn-out hill-climb, where accurate positions are hard to obtain more than once an hour. He never won the Targa Florio, the oldest road race in the world, but there can be little doubt that he did more than most to add to its character. Competing four times in the late twenties (a period rich in great drivers of the old and new schools—Nuvolari, Varzi, Costantini, Wagner, Campari, Divo, Boillot, Goux), he twice finished second, once third and once fourth.

After his fourth French G.P. victory, 1947

As a member of the Bugatti team, which was then under the management of Costantini, Chiron made his first appearance in the Targa Florio in 1928. For three successive years the cars from Alsace had won the Sicilian race and this year, with such drivers as Divo, Conelli, Minoia, Madame Junek, Dreyfus, Foresti and a relative newcomer named Nuvolari, their chances seemed high against the Alfa Romeos and the Maseratis. The race was run over what is known as the medium circuit, shortened from 90 to 67 miles, the highest point being through picturesque Polizzi, 3,000 feet above sea level. Florio's decision that five laps should be covered, giving a total distance of 335½ miles, brought protests from some drivers, who said that this would be a test beyond human endurance. Divo and Campari were the outstanding figures in the race; the Frenchman with the Bugatti started after the Italian with the Alfa Romeo, but gradually caught him up and passed him to win by nearly two minutes and at an average speed of 45·6 m.p.h. As a newcomer, Chiron did extraordinarily well, losing only seven minutes to the winner; after crossing the line for the fifth time, he flashed past the pits without stopping and began to climb into the mountains again—it was only after noticing that the crews at the little wayside tyre stations were packing up and preparing to go home that he realized he must be on a sixth lap! So after covering a distance which the veterans had declared impossible, he sought out Vincenzo Florio and inquired angrily 'Why did you not wave a flag to tell me I had finished?'

Chiron's greatest year in the Targa Florio came in 1930. For five successive years Bugatti had been unbeaten. But the Italians were determined to break the spell. The Alfa Romeos were technically advanced and their team included Nuvolari, Campari and Maggi; while Varzi, independently, entered his revamped and potent P.2 in opposition as much to the works as to others. Varzi's handling of the pure racing machine was marvellous. Starting 12 minutes behind Chiron, he gained 1 minute on him during the first twenty miles and broke the lap record by nearly 4 minutes. With only half a lap to go, the two men were practically equal on time, so far as could be calculated. But in the last wild descent from Polizzi, Chiron's mechanic, a youth from the factory in a race for the first time, became groggy and rolled about helplessly in his seat. Chiron tried to put some life into him by shouting and hitting him—a distraction which was his undoing, for he slid on loose gravel into the outer retaining wall at a bend, breaking the left front wheel and tearing the spare from its support. The broken wheel, the jack and the tools were left on the road once the spare was on and Chiron drove away in a frenzy towards the finishing line, 25 miles away. But immediately behind him there was another drama. Varzi was low on petrol and at a wayside station, he ordered his mechanic to pour another can into the tank while the engine was still running; some of it reached the hot exhaust and flames began to lick the tail. That traditional aide, a cushion, was used to beat it out and now Varzi tore for the line. Chiron was the first across it, but because of the individual starts it was not certain that he had won. The minutes and the seconds ticked by and then it was seen that Varzi was the winner by less than two minutes after nearly seven hours running. The Bugatti grip on the race had been broken, despite Chiron's magnificent drive, one of his greatest races.

After the First World War, European cars and drivers had met with

Bugatti days, Brooklands, 1927

little success at Indianapolis. Ballot tried and managed to finish second. Mercedes, Fiat and Bugatti were all unsuccessful. Then, in 1929, Chiron decided to make an attempt with one of the 1926–7 1·5-litre supercharged G.P. Delages. Totally ignorant of American conditions, he allowed himself a month to train on the Hoosier track. But the car which had been so successful under European conditions was not so brilliant in the '500'—altogether the Delage spent 16 min. 40 sec. at the pits for routine tyre and fuel stops and also with magneto trouble, and finally securing seventh position out of 33 starters. It was rather disappointing; like other Europeans, before and since, Chiron returned from Indianapolis realizing that the '500' was unlike any other race and required a specially-built car and special training.

Right at the other end of the racing scale from the complications of the apparently simple American classic came the Monaco G.P. In the twenties the A.C. de Monaco had no international standing and had to be satisfied to figure as a branch of the Nice club. Resenting this, Antony Noghès proposed that a real race should be held through the hilly, winding streets of the Principality. It was a daring move, for there was still an idea that safety could only be assured only as cars spread themselves round a fairly long circuit, certainly not after a mass start on a fairly narrow street, but the idea of a Monaco race was translated into reality. It was a huge success from the beginning, the first race, in 1929, being won by Williams on a Bugatti, at an average of just under 50 m.p.h. No accidents marred the day.

Intensely interested in this spectacular race through the streets of his native town, Chiron was present in 1930 as a member of the Bugatti team. His greatest competition came from his team-mate Dreyfus. Driving brilliantly, Chiron successively reduced the lap record from 2 min 15 sec to 2 min 8 sec. Dreyfus got to within 2 min 2 sec of him but could not improve on this. Feeling that his crash helmet was hindering him, Chiron pulled it off and flung it away while climbing the hill to the Casino. Occasional spluttering indicated that his fuel supply was running low; at the pits, ten litres were dumped into the tank and the Monaco favourite got away still in the lead to begin his last lap with victory in sight. At the station hairpin, however, things went wrong, for Chiron found that he had no control over the carburetter. When he wanted full opening, the engine shut off and when he wanted to slow down it opened up. Subsequent examination showed that the throttle stop had broken off. Chiron crossed the line with despairing gestures, in second place and having lost the lap record by one second.

In 1931 the new twin-camshaft Bugattis were ready and were entrusted to Chiron, Varzi, Divo and Bouriat. For twenty rounds Varzi kept the lead, but Chiron took it from him when the Italian punctured (then ran on the rim until the wheel disintegrated and amid a shower of sparks, continued on the brake drum to the pits). Chiron, Varzi and Fagioli all equalled the previous year's record of 2 minutes 7 seconds but it was with the fairly substantial margin of 3 minutes that Chiron was acclaimed the winner.

Two months later the French Grand Prix was held at Montlhéry on a ten-hour basis. Taking the wheel at the start, Chiron appeared to be in excellent form and aroused the enthusiasm of the spectators by diving down from the top of the embankment to pass slower competitors. There were three strong teams among the twenty-three starters—

Winner on home ground, 1931

Bugatti, Maserati and Alfa Romeo. On the road portion of the track brakes were put to a severe test and in this respect the Bugattis had an advantage, for the wheel and brake drum formed a unit and even shoes could be changed in a few seconds. For a time Fagioli's Maserati kept the lead, then Varzi, taking over from Chiron, shot ahead on the Bugatti; out of the twenty-three starters only twelve finished, Chiron–Varzi combination winning with a distance of 782·1 miles.

Travelling further afield, Chiron finished second on Nürburgring, at Montenero and Pescara in Italy and rounded off the year by winning the Czechoslovak Grand Prix for Bugatti.

The year 1932 was a busy one which opened badly. At Monaco, when being chased hard by Nuvolari, Chiron came down to the Chicane to find the road blocked by a car out of control, the result being a triple roll which nearly ended in the sea and personal injuries. These, how-ever, were not sufficiently serious to prevent coming to the line in the Targa Florio a month later; once again he failed in his ambition to win the gold plate, but as usual he made a brilliant display, finishing third behind Nuvolari and Borzacchini, both on Alfa Romeos.

Teaming with Varzi on the 4,900-c.c. Bugattis, he met with no success in the Monza race on June 5th, both cars going out with engine trouble. The French Grand Prix on July 3 was run on the fast Rheims circuit and was won by Nuvolari on Alfa Romeo at the fast average of 92·26 m.p.h. For a short time Varzi got the lead, but this so inflamed the fiery Nuvolari that he put in a lap at 99·5 m.p.h., finishing first with Borzacchini second, Caracciola third and Chiron fourth. The ill-luck continued. In the German Grand Prix on Nürburgring Varzi was un-able to start owing to eye trouble; Chiron soon had ignition failure, then broke his goggles with slight injury to his eyes and finally the rear axle refused further service. In the Monza Grand Prix, where there were three heats and a final, Chiron could not do better than sixth. Then, once again at the end of the season, he made up for this by finishing first in the Czechoslovak Grand Prix with the 2,300-c.c. Bugatti.

In 1933, having broken with Bugatti, Chiron teamed with Caracciola to drive a pair of Alfas. But again the season opened badly, for while practising at Monaco for the Scuderia C.C.'s first race, the German driver skidded and sustained such injuries that he was unable to drive for a year; in the event Chiron finishing fourth behind Varzi, Borzacchini and Dreyfus. In the Belgian 24-hour race he secured first position. Then came three more firsts in succession: at Miramas, Brno and San Sebastian. Rounding off the season at Monza he broke the lap record at 113·9 m.p.h. but just failed to finish.

The 1934 Grand Prix at Monaco was Chiron's greatest disappointment. In his Alfa Romeo he had led practically the whole race, followed by Moll in a similar B2900, when his steering gear broke on the last lap, opposite Monte Carlo station. From time to time the broken stud took hold and by reducing speed Chiron was able to cross the line and finish second 1 minute 2 seconds behind the young Franco-Algerian. A week later came the Mille Miglia and a third place behind Varzi and Nuvolari. Then to Tripoli in North Africa, where the Grand Prix had taken its place among the important races; in this Grand Prix Chiron took third place and the lap record at 124·4 m.p.h.

Race followed race in quick succession in this year of Grand Prix revolution: Chiron was first at Casablanca; out with mechanical trouble in the Avusrennen, third in the Eifelrennen, first in the French Grand Prix at Montlhéry, third in the German Grand Prix, out in Belgium after having led by a minute, fifth in Switzerland and Spain and fourth in the Italian Grand Prix.

In the 1935 Monaco Grand Prix Chiron had to be satisfied with fifth place on his Alfa Romeo. A week later he again failed in his ambition to win the Targa Florio, his Alfa Romeo being preceded by Brivio's machine of the same make. Driving the twin-engined Alfa Romeo he secured fifth place in the Tripoli Grand Prix, second on the Avus track and then the same position on the Eifel circuit. Ten other events were of secondary importance and mechanical troubles forced him out on five other occasions.

Mercedes-Benz secured the services of the Monégasque champion in 1936 but ill-luck dogged this move and he was unhappy with the short-chassis W.25. The Monaco Grand Prix, run in unusual conditions of pouring rain, was marked by a sensational pile-up at the chicane from which Chiron emerged without much damage to himself or his machine, but was unable to restart the engine. On the fast Tripoli circuit his practice times were impressive, but a broken accelerator control forced him out of the race, at Tunis the petrol pumps were defective and he was obliged to retire from the Hungarian Grand Prix at Budapest. In the German Grand Prix he overturned with much damage to his machine and less to himself. He did not race the German cars again.

He went into semi-retirement in 1937, appearing only once with a Talbot to win the sports-car French Grand Prix at Montlhéry. Then, before the Second World War put an end to motor racing in Europe, he had some trial runs with the Auto Union team, but did not race at all in 1939.

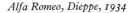
Alfa Romeo, Dieppe, 1934

Called up for military service on the outbreak of war, he managed to secure demobilization on the collapse of France. When Hitler decided that there should be no more free zone, Chiron considered it prudent to step over the frontier into Switzerland. He found an outlet for his devouring activity in the dangerous and daring task of smuggling Allied airmen out of neutral Switzerland into occupied France, then across the Pyrenees to Spain and England.

After the war the revival of motor racing was slow. Cars were scarce; many of the old drivers had disappeared. With his pre-war Talbot, Chiron was under a real handicap and only occasionally came home the winner. Most notably, he won the first post-war French Grand Prix at Lyon and also raced at Jersey, appeared several times at Silverstone and brought his heavy car into second place in 1948 Monaco Grand Prix.

A sensational experience at Syracuse shook even his strong nerves— at more than 100 m.p.h. his car burst into flames. The scene was impressed on his mind with lightning rapidity: switch off, engage third, prepare to leave the car. But when only a couple of inches from the ground he realized that he was travelling much too fast to drop with safety. Just ahead was a bend and a cemetery; the gate was open; bales of straw were on the bend. It must be a crash. He hauled himself back into the burning car and crashed.

When he was 56 years old, Chiron drove in his last Grand Prix, at Monaco, and finished sixth in a works V-8 Lancia. Then, in 1959 he took second place in his class in the last Mille Miglia with a Citroen DS19.

During his long racing career Chiron also took part in eleven Monte Carlo Rallies, starting from various points in Europe; in 1954 he started from his home town in a Lancia—and won, thus becoming the only man to win both of the Principality's classic events.

On his sixtieth birthday, Louis Chiron decided to hang up his crash helmet, his goggles and his gloves. But it was not to go into retirement. On the initiative of Prince Rainier, he was nominated *commissaire général* (general manager) of the Monte Carlo races and the Rally. His competence could not be doubted; his vitality was unlimited. And to this his varied interests on behalf of race drivers, his official position on numerous committees, his duties as a Consul, and he is indeed a busy man. It is hardly surprising that he has no real hobbies—indeed, his only pastime, when he needs something to pass the time, is cooking (and it is said that on occasion he surpasses the professional cook aboard Prince Rainier's yacht!).

Louis Chiron's characteristics as a racing driver can be summarized in the one word 'Enthusiasm'. More than any other man he gave the impression of *joie de vivre* when he took the wheel of a car for a long-distance race, a hill-climb, a sprint (or even in a mere rally). Unlike certain other leading drivers he had no very distinctive style, but one could not help being struck by the fact that he appeared to be really enjoying himself when in competition. He liked 'traffic'—driving on a short circuit with many competitors around him or within sight. The old-time long-distance races over a road circuit, where one rarely caught sight of a competitor, had little appeal for him. By the same token, he looked upon record breaking as dull sport.

To the Germans in the thirties he was 'the Wily Fox'; to many others over the years he was 'the Perfectionist'—two sobriquets which summed up his mastery of tactics and his delicate, polished style of driving.

Talbot, Lyon, 1947

Happy veteran (Maserati, Berne) 1950

The principal racing successes of **LOUIS CHIRON**

1926	1st:	Comminges G.P.
1927	2nd:	A.C.F. f.l. Race, Montlhéry.
1928	1st:	Italian G.P.; Spanish G.P.; Antibes G.P.; Marne G.P.; Rome G.P.; San Sebastian G.P.
1929	1st:	German G.P.; San Sebastian G.P.
1930	1st:	Belgian G.P.; Lyons G.P.
	2nd:	Monaco G.P.; Targa Fario.
1931	1st:	French G.P.; Monaco G.P.; Masaryk G.P.
	2nd:	German G.P.; Coppa Ciano; Coppa Acerbo.
1932	1st:	Dieppe G.P.; Masaryk G.P.; Nice Circuit.
	3rd:	Targa Florio; Coppa Acerbo.
1933	1st:	Spanish G.P.; Marseilles G.P.; Masaryk G.P.; Spa 24-hour Race.
1934	1st:	French G.P.; Marne G.P.
	2nd:	Monaco G.P.; Spanish G.P.; Alessandria f.l. Race; Algerian G.P.
	3rd:	German G.P.; Eifelrennen; Mille Miglia; Tripoli G.P.

1935	1st:	Lorraine G.P.
	2nd:	Dieppe G.P.; Marne G.P.; Nice G.P.; Avusrennen; Circuit of Biella; Targa Florio.
	3rd:	Belgian G.P.; Masaryk G.P.; Eifelrennen.
1937	1st:	French G.P.
1946	2nd:	St. Cloud G.P.
	3rd:	Coupe de Paris.
1947	1st:	French G.P.; Comminges G.P.
	2nd:	Marne G.P.; Nice G.P.; Jersey International Road Race.
1948	2nd:	Paris G.P.; Monaco G.P.
	3rd:	Comminges G.P.; Penya Rhin G.P.
1949	1st:	G.P. de France.
1950	3rd:	Monaco G.P.
1951	3rd:	Albi G.P.; Monza Sports Car Race.
1953	2nd:	Sables d'Olonne G.P.; Syracuse G.P.
1956	3rd:	Autumn Cup, Montlhéry

1935 hey-day

LUIGI FAGIOLI

by RODNEY WALKERLEY

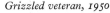

WHEN he died, three weeks after his accident in the tunnel at Monte Carlo in 1952, Luigi Fagioli was one of the very few veterans of pre-war motor racing still active. He was 54. This rugged Italian had begun his long career with the little 1,100-c.c. Salmson of 1926, after which he moved into first-class racing with Maseratis and the monoposto Alfa Romeos of the early thirties and he reached the heights with the super-powerful Mercedes-Benz and Auto Unions in the 1934–9 era when Grand Prix racing produced a glamour and spectacle never seen before —or since.

Fagioli was short, stocky, swarthy, with close-cropped receding hair that, when he was in his forties, was turning grey. His bullet head sat aggressively on an almost indiscernible neck. Broad shoulders and muscular, hairy arms told of great physical strength. He was indeed a man in the mould of the pioneer drivers who wrestled with the monster cars at the turn of the century, when sheer strength was at least as essential as driving skill. He scowled more often than he laughed, he was taciturn and quick to fury. Like so many Italian racing men of his time he was a true tiger in action, driving with a dash and determination matching the skill that came of so many years behind the wheel, in a period when no quarter was given or asked. He had the ruthlessness of a Farina—without Farina's contemptuous calm at the wheel—but it was very rare for Fagioli to leave the road.

He was, I think, a man consumed with ambition, not untinged with jealousy; he had few friends on the circuits. It was a temperament that led to a rivalry little removed from open hatred for men like Rudolf Caracciola and Achille Varzi. This antipathy for Caracciola, leader of the Mercedes team, coloured the last years before the war and was matched only by the jealousy of Hermann Lang, Fagioli's one-time chief mechanic who replaced him in the team (and Caracciola in his hatred).

He was undoubtedly one of the great drivers in an epoch of great drivers, even if his style was more brutal than polished. He habitually drove on the limit, even against team orders, and frequently put a wheel on the grass or scraped a kerb or the straw bales on a corner.

From the start of a racing career that continued for twenty-eight years Fagioli was rarely out of the first three or four—if his car lasted. His strategy was to keep close to the leaders, harrying them until, as the race entered its last and decisive phase and the field, as usual, began to thin out, he would slam his foot down and drive faster and faster. Although he won many races, he recorded the fastest lap only three times—on the long Masaryk Ring, near Brno, round the fast Bremgarten circuit at Berne and through the streets of Monaco, in the only race in which he both took fastest lap and won (in 1935 with the Mercedes).

He began winning races in 1930 with a Maserati and for three years he remained faithful to the Maserati brothers of Bologna. He won for

Grizzled veteran, 1950

87

Maserati days (Monaco, 1931)

them the Grand Prix of Monza (1931), beating Borzacchini's Alfa Romeo and Varzi's Bugatti, and the Prix de Rome on the Littorio circuit, but it was becoming all too clear that the small Maserati factory could no longer compete with the challenge of the new P.3 monoposto Alfa Romeo.

In 1933, the last season of what amounted to Free Formula racing, he therefore joined Enzo Ferrari to drive in the team of Alfa Romeos which he was operating on behalf of the factory and that year he won the Grand Prix of Comminges, at St. Gaudens, driving against Jean-Pierre Wimille and his protégé, Guy Moll, on older Alfa Romeos. In the Coppa Acerbo, the long 320-mile race at Pescara, he snatched victory from the great Tazio Nuvolari, then driving a Maserati as an independent. Three second places in races won by Louis Chiron's Alfa Romeo brought Fagioli enough points to win him the Championship of Italy and the invitation to join the new Mercedes-Benz team which marked the return of the Germans to Grand Prix racing under the 1934 750-kilogramme Formula.

Germany was then—as since—short of first-class drivers with Grand Prix experience. In fact, only Caracciola could claim that status. Driving his white Alfa Romeo he had beaten Fagioli in his first race against him, the 1932 Monza Grand Prix. Then, at Easter, 1933, he had crashed badly, when his brakes failed in practice at Monte Carlo, and he broke his hip, an injury from which he never fully recovered. And he was, of course, a champion driver of the big Mercedes sports cars. Mercedes, whose third driver was the debonair exhibitionist Manfred von Brauchitsch, a young and impetuous driver of little experience, therefore needed Fagioli, as the only available top ranking driver, for Nuvolari, Varzi and Chiron were already under contract elsewhere.

Fagioli accepted the engagement with eagerness, for it meant a highly-paid wheel in one of the two German teams that were equipped with the most expensive racing cars ever made, backed by a racing department organized regardless of cost (it is estimated that both Auto

Winning for Mercedes-Benz (and, of course, for Fagioli!) 1934 Spanish Grand Prix

Union and Mercedes spent £1 million over five racing years at the pre-war sterling rate).

Caracciola was naturally Number One in the team. Fagioli, 34-year-old veteran, felt himself shut out, driving to team orders so that the victory should go to the German. Several other Germans, including Henne, the champion motor cycle rider, were tried with no success. Fagioli was to be the main support if anything interfered with Caracciola or von Brauchitsch, and Caracciola was always in pain when he drove.

Now began the feud between the two men. The cars were always raced under Alfred Neubauer's strict orders but Fagioli was obsessed with the idea that he could always out-drive his team-mates and to Neubauer's fury, harried Caracciola in race after race, forcing the German to go unnecessarily fast, or disregarded orders and passed him. That first year of 1934 Fagioli won the Coppa Acerbo again, once more beating Nuvolari's much slower Maserati, and he won the Spanish Grand Prix at San Sebastian, beating Caracciola again and Nuvolari (now mounted on the new 3·3-litre Bugatti) as well. It was the last Grand Prix of the year, and Fagioli was determined to snatch the laurel wreath from his rival. Well in the lead, Caracciola eased up on signals from the Mercedes pit; Fagioli did not. The Germans resented this attitude, but they could not dispense with Fagioli. The standing arrangement was that Germans should win wherever possible except in Italy, where it was agreed Fagioli could drive his own race and win if he could.

A few weeks before the Spanish race there had been the Italian Grand Prix at Monza where a ridiculous little circuit had been laid out, with chicanes, making a lap of only 2·6 miles which had to be covered 116 times, offering the drivers 310 miles with 1,600 slow corners. The affair was more exhausting to men and machines than even the unique race at Monaco. On his home ground Fagioli shot into the lead but then had supercharger trouble that forced him to retire, leaving Hans Stuck (Auto Union) and Caracciola first and second. Before half-distance Caracciola tired, Fagioli took over the car and, when Stuck refuelled and changed wheels, roared into the lead and won easily—this helped to convince him he was a faster man than the German.

The following year, 1935, at the Spa-Francorchamps circuit, fastest in Europe, for the Belgian Grand Prix, Fagioli was solemnly warned not to disregard his r.p.m. limits or his orders to keep behind Caracciola unless the German was forced to slow. Fagioli, in surly mood, dutifully obeyed but closed up on to Caracciola's tail. For half an hour he was breathing down the German's neck and, when he brought in his car for the first pit stop, his rage boiled over. He got out of the Mercedes, tore off his linen helmet and goggles, flung them into the pit and stalked away in a fury. In the pit Neubauer was shrieking for von Brauchitsch, who had already retired and was, in fact, asleep in the sun behind the pits. Thus the result read: first, Caracciola; second, Fagioli-von Brauchitsch.

That summer he nevertheless added to his stature. He won the dangerous Avus race, at 148 m.p.h. for 122 miles, beating Chiron's Bimotore Alfa Romeo, won the Monaco Grand Prix and beat Caracciola in the Penya Rhin race round Barcelona's Montjuich Park. Twice again he ran second to Caracciola—in the Swiss and Spanish races.

Relations between the two great drivers were going from bad to

G

worse. Now, when Caracciola was in the lead and the signal was to hold position, he watched his mirrors for Fagioli and, if he saw the irascible Italian closing, would open up again at the risk of the two men blowing up each other's cars.

The next season, 1936, was disastrous for Mercedes-Benz, with their new, short-chassis versions of the W.25. Louis Chiron had joined the team and later in the season, Hermann Lang, Fagioli's chief mechanic, was given a drive; he at once displayed such speed and control that he became a permanent member of the team and immediately challenged Caracciola as the fastest driver. Thus were sown the seeds of another feud that was to continue when Fagioli had left the stage. The cars were fast but unreliable and Auto Union, with even more power from their rear-mounted V-16 engines, were strengthened by the amazing virtuosity of young Bernd Rosemeyer, a born champion.

In the Monaco race that year Fagioli had one of his rare accidents. Ordered, for once, to increase speed in support of Caracciola, who was hard pressed by Nuvolari's Alfa Romeo, he drove through a storm of rain faster and faster and then slid out of control, on sand that had been sprinkled on spilt oil, and crashed.

At Tripoli, however, it was Fagioli who saved Mercedes by finishing third behind Varzi and Stuck on Auto Unions.

At the end of the season his contract was terminated, and he promptly joined the Auto Union team, which had been weakened by what amounted to the defection of Achille Varzi (who had taken the downward path of women and drugs and was quite unable to drive a 520 b.h.p. Auto Union).

Now, in 1937, the hatred of Fagioli for Caracciola was not only in the open but the men were in opposing camps. Matters came to a head at the Tripoli Grand Prix, then the fastest road race in the world, run at over 130 m.p.h. on a circuit of successive full-throttle curves and one short straight past the pits and stands. Lang won the race at over 134 m.p.h., with Auto Unions second, third and fourth.

Fagioli, raging and shaking his fist, harried Caracciola, unable to pass. He claimed afterwards that the German deliberately blocked him lap after lap, which was probably true. Just before the finish Fagioli slammed his Auto Union past to snatch fifth place, Caracciola sixth. The German had left his car and was sitting in the pits when Fagioli, beside himself with fury, snatched up a wheel hammer and flung it at Caracciola's head. According to my friend Lazlo Hartmann, the Hungarian driver, he followed this up by hurling himself at Caracciola with an open jack-knife from the pit counter!

After that when it came to the 160 m.p.h. Avus race, Neubauer announced that if Fagioli and Caracciola were drawn in the same heat, Mercedes would not race. By coincidence, it did not arise. At the end of that season Fagioli abandoned racing and so never handled the new 3-litre cars of 1938.

In 1950, however, at the age of 50, now grey-haired, his face lined, and his temper much less uncontrollable, he came back (as one of the 'Three Fs') in the Alfa Romeo team of 1½-litre supercharged cars. He willingly acknowledged Juan Fangio as team leader, and finished second to the New Master in three races and behind team mate Farina, World Champion, in a fourth. Faithful to his old friends the Maserati brothers, he drove their 1,100-c.c. Osca in the Mille Miglia, finishing seventh and, in 1951, won the 1,100-c.c. class for them. That year,

Swiss Grand Prix, 1950

sharing a car with Fangio he was co-winner of the French Grand Prix at Rheims. In 1952 he finished third in Mille Miglia with a Lancia, beating Caracciola (Mercedes) once again. Then he was to drive a small Lancia Aurielia saloon in the curtain raiser event at Monte Carlo. During an early morning practice, the 54-year-old veteran touched a kerb in the long, curving tunnel, zig-zagged from wall to wall and crashed. Three weeks later he died from his injuries.

He was mourned by all who knew him, for he was a great man in an age of great drivers.

The principal of racing successes of **LUIGI FAGIOLI**

1926	3rd:	Circuit of Florence.
1927	2nd:	Voiturette Targa Florio.
1928	2nd:	Circuit of Senigallia.
1929	2nd:	Circuit of Three Provinces, Bologna; Tripoli Voiturette Race.
1930	1st:	Coppa Principe di Piemonte; Coppa Ciano; Coppa Castelli Romani.
1931	1st:	Monza G.P.
	2nd:	Monaco G.P.; Tunis G.P.
	3rd:	Coppa Ciano.
1932	1st:	Circuit of Senigallia.
	2nd:	Italian G.P.; Masaryk G.P.; Monza G.P.; Rome G.P.; Circuit of Bolsena.
	3rd:	Monaco G.P.; Coppa Principe di Piemonte.

1933	1st:	Italian G.P.; Comminges G.P.; Coppa Acerbo.
	2nd:	Spanish G.P.; Marseilles G.P.; Masaryk G.P.
1934	1st:	Italian G.P.; Spanish G.P.
	2nd:	German G.P.; Masaryk G.P.
1935	1st:	Monaco G.P.; Coppa Acerbo; Avusrennen; Penya Rhin G.P.
	2nd:	Belgian G.P.; Swiss G.P.
	3rd:	Tripoli G.P.
1936	3rd:	Tripoli G.P.
1950	2nd:	Belgian G.P.; British G.P.; French G.P.; Swiss G.P.
	3rd:	Italian G.P.
1951	1st:	French G.P.
1952	3rd:	Mille Miglia.

Bergmeister, 1937

HANS STUCK

by JERRY SLONIGER

Shelsley Walsh, 1930 . . .

. . . and with the BMW 507 in 1959

THREE decades is an honourable span for any career—but when the daily bread is earned at the wheel of a works racing car, thirty-four professional seasons are little short of sensational. Hans Stuck started fairly late too, driving his first private event in a Dürkopp at the age 24 and turning to full-time racing at 27, 'when my farm failed'. Stuck was to be a farmer if his parents had any say in the matter, but the banks and an uncanny sense for motorized hill-climbing were against them.

Stuck's first victory stemmed from a private wager, his first amateur entry in 1924 led to a class win, and his last full season at the age of 60 brought him the German Mountain Championship. In between he was a Grand Prix ace, both record holder and class champion in power boat racing, a competition skier and even licensed ski instructor, and six-handicap golfer, all more or less in passing!

Many sources, Press and otherwise, insist Hans Stuck is even older than he says—he claims December 27, 1900 as his birth date, Warsaw as the place. His parents were on a business trip in Poland. The controversy arose because Stuck is credited with being an artillery officer in the First World War. At 17? Hans himself says simply, 'I was a very young lieutenant'. Others claim he must have been older—and there are no definitive records available from Poland now. At the other end of his career it is hard enough to accept that he won a national title at 60 without bowing to claims he was really born in 1895 or even 1890; young-looking and obviously vigorous Hans certainly is but it seems hardly likely that he quit racing weekly at 70 (or even 65). But then his entire career was touched with fantasy.

One ghost should be laid to rest immediately—Hans is plain Stuck, without a von before his name, all race literature of the thirties to the contrary. The driver's mother was the last of a Huguenot line by the name of Villiez and Hans was granted the right as a youth to be officially known as Stuck von Villiez, a common enough concession to family trees in those days.

When he began to appear regularly in a racing cockpit the name was simply too long for race programme typesetters who dropped the Villiez and misplaced the von, most often in England. His double citizenship no doubt contributed to this mix-up. Hans carried an Austrian passport into the Second World War, one memento of his days with the Austro-Daimler team, though his family came from the Freiburg area of Germany and his estate lay south of Munich on German soil. He still had this Austrian citizenship after the war and thus returned to racing sooner than his German colleagues.

Stuck actually finished his first 'race' backwards, but it was as fully planned as any later hill victory in his long career. The young estate owner had circumvented a parental no-motoring ban by pointing out that his milk would be sold fresh if he bought a car and delivered it to Munich himself. Enter Dürkopp number one, a semi-sports model.

93

There is some suspicion he paid far more attention to carving seconds off his farm-to-Munich time than to the milk he carried because this first car was soon followed by a sports Dürkopp.

As a member of the landed gentry of his area Stuck naturally fell into motoring debates with other leading citizens who scoffed at his speed boasts for the 'tiny' Dürkopp of two seats and two litres. So, in a rash moment, Stuck bet he could climb a certain hill on the way to Munich faster backwards than they could with their big tourers pointing in the proper direction.

Stuck's reputation for out-thinking his opposition was naturally embryonic then so they gave him three full weeks to make ready. Hans had his gearbox reversed, giving four speeds backwards, put in a little practice and won. This led to an entry in the Baden-Baden hill-climb (gearbox back in its rightful position) with his friends to cheer him on and thus he won his first formal competition (in the 2-litre class). Seven started, two finished but, he notes dryly, 'I won and that's all they remember today'. That Dürkopp had 60 h.p. but as racing fever had become stronger than parental wishes he soon had it tuned to match factory models, until it produced some 80 h.p. and 100 m.p.h. He could soon boast of a year with four hill-climb wins in a row, mostly on loose-surfaced courses.

The Stuck approach to hill-climbs didn't vary much over thirty-six years of racing. For a climb he didn't know Hans drove up the hill slowly, on occasion as many as a hundred times, but never walked the course—'You learn the wrong line that way'. Thus by the time official practice opened he often had a week or more of slow practice. On a hill like historical Schauinsland outside Freiburg, perennial site of the German national championship run, Stuck knows the corners like his own driveway. He only drove Schauinsland twenty or thirty times each year before training there. There was no question of a poor memory either. This is a man who will bet he can drive a piece of open road once and then name every salient feature, bridge or tree. Of official practice, Stuck says, 'My first run was usually too fast, the second about right to win. If there was time for a third or fourth they were just for polish'.

This absolute concentration led to his new career when the farm failed in 1927, along with a good many other businesses. Hans looked around and decided racing was a good profession. So he became a race driver. Just like that—as he tells the tale it sounds logical. Stuck went to Austro-Daimler and to their 3-litre overhead-camshaft, (100 b.h.p. at 4000 r.p.m.) ADM. This car was really a Porsche design, though the Professor had left for Daimler-Benz by that time, and in fact Stuck was to spend much of his career in Porsche designs.

Austro-Daimler could hardly help liking their towering newcomer who won seven runs his first season and had fastest time of the day in four of them, regardless of class. In the four seasons he raced the Austrian cars Stuck won a total of forty-three races, earning the Swiss mountain title for 1928, the Austrian the following year and the European hill-climb crown for racing cars in 1930, his final season with Austro-Daimler. A.D. even entered him for the Monaco Grand Prix of 1929 with a stripped touring model (although he did not start in the race) and he spent winter week-ends on the Eibsee and Titisee lakes in ice races and special matches against Udet and his Klemm sports plane —five laps for Stuck, seven for Udet.

With Auto Union, French Grand Prix, 1934

Thinking about the 1938 car, Nürburgring

Hans gets a special gleam when ice racing is mentioned but he really thinks it is more fun without spiked tyres. He drove by the seat of his pants (one reason he wasn't all that fond of the front-cockpit Auto Unions) and obviously had an extra measure of sensitivity for tricky surfaces. He liked fast tracks for circuit racing—Tripoli or Spa—better than the twisty ones, despite his hill-climb talent, and found Nürburgring too tiring for drivers. Airfield courses are 'simply stupid'.

In 1931, to split hairs, he was only semi-professional, for virtually nobody had full works backing but special drivers like Stuck could buy a Mercedes SSK at bargain rates and the Untertürkheim plant would keep it up to par as they went along. That was enough for Stuck who already had his hill-climb system down pat—'do all the braking and gear changing before the bend, then stay on the loud pedal all the way around'.

Stuck's SSK was raced up the same mountains as his Austro-Daimler and generally gave him a new record by breaking the one he had set the year before. Hans won his first big circuit race in 1931 too, the Lemberg G.P., and then on his thirty-first birthday left for Argentina with the SSK to run in their Grand Prix. The German visitor took one look at the roads, found that there was not even minimum ground clearance for his Mercedes and promptly withdrew. He did agree to enter the Brazilian mountain championship race from Rio to Petropolis—probably the longest 'hill-climb' on record since it covered some 37 miles, large portions of which were flat. Stuck won—a near-redundant comment when it came to mountain racing.

The six-foot-two German won so often over the thirty-six years he raced privately and professionally that his trophies were crowding the family out of their Garmisch mountain home. Hans had the lesser silverware melted down and made into table-tops, engraved with data from the cups themselves—data such as his International Alpine Championship for 1932, in the sports car class. This new title covered old familiar events with names of special honour in climbing: Stilfser Joch, Kesselberg, Mont Ventoux, Klausenpass, Wuergauer, Freiburg, Lueckendorf, Gaisberg—all were Stuck victories.

The hill-climb tally continued but Hans Stuck went on to bigger racing in 1933 when he joined Auto Union to be their Number One driver when the 750-kg. Grand Prix formula came into effect in 1934. That season was destined to be Stuck's finest in a long career. He opened it in March with international records for 100 miles, 200 kilometres and one hour (at 134·9 m.p.h.) with the Auto Union at Berlin's Avus (then without its high-banked wall). By the end of 1934 he had won the German and Swiss Grands Prix, the Czech Masaryk race, finished second in two more classics, was fourth in Spain and won four climbs. To ice the cake Stuck captured five new records at the Avus late in the year, using a partially streamlined 4·3 litre 295 b.h.p. Auto Union and covering 100 kilometres at better than 150 m.p.h.

If a world championship had been awarded in 1934 the winner would have been Hans Stuck, a man who drove by his instincts, yet beat the conventional Mercedes with probably the worst-handling and least sensitive of all the Auto Unions. His German G.P. win at the Ring, a circuit which he in any case disliked, was one of his finest, involving as it did a long battle with Caracciola (Mercedes) in the early stages and then hanging on with a less than perfect engine to finish the 350-mile race safely ahead of the Fagioli Mercedes.

In mid-February of 1935 Hans did a flying mile in Italy at very nearly 200 m.p.h. under the worst of weather conditions, but the rest of that year was neither Stuck's nor Auto Union's. Hans managed a sole win at Monza but he again captured the German mountain title, virtually his for the entering.

From his peak of 1934 to the outbreak of war, Stuck seemed to drive in the shadow of the Rosemeyer legend—and there is no doubt the mercurial Bernd had a special feel for the brutal tail-waggers—except on Stuck's beloved mountains. He remained a team driver up to the start of the Second World War and in 1937 at Freiburg, for instance, demonstrated his absolute mastery of the uphill sprint, yet again. The lower portion of Schauinsland was still wet as they climbed: Lang in 8 minutes 29 seconds for Mercedes, Caracciola in 8 minutes 17 seconds in a sister car. Before the cheers could die Rosemeyer, the golden boy, did 8 minutes 11 seconds in an Auto Union and that seemed to be that—or so everybody but Hans Stuck believed. Using twin rear wheels, but even more his uncanny concentration, Stuck took another second off the day's record time and once again ruled the mountain.

On the Grand Prix side, Stuck felt a little left out at Auto Union, so he borrowed a racing engine and fitted it to a brutal hydroplane driven by a worm gear in a tube. With its massive doses of power the boat started slowly but ran like a berserk whale when it got moving, fast enough for a world record in the class and still another German championship, this time for lake racing without the icy coating. Stuck's chief memory of this beast was the problem he faced when lapping the field. The slightest wave, much less another big boat's wake, was enough to sink not only their hopes but their hero as well if not handled perfectly. His finger-tip feel triumphed though and when the war came Stuck still had his water toy which he hid on Lake Constance where it was found by a French army unit after the war. They couldn't make the alcohol-fuelled engine work so Stuck was hauled over from his post-war Arlberg retreat and told to make it run. Hans did, turned a few 'laps' for his own amusement, then listened with horror as a French lieutenant announced he would now drive the monster. Despite Stuck's pleas and dire warnings about its behaviour at the slightest ripple if not ridden with a firm hand, the Frenchman sallied forth, to hit a wavelet at a speed far beyond his talents, capsize and drown. The boat still lies in the lake and Stuck was jailed briefly, 'for sabotage'.

Apart from boating he was also booked as driver for the now legendary Daimler-Benz record car which never ran. The government wanted a steady hand at the wheel and the Land Speed Record would be a fine retirement present. Besides Stuck and Ferdinand Porsche had been friends for years. That project of course fell prey to history and the outbreak of war.

Thoughts of his retirement were also premature. Immediately after the war Stuck returned to the winner's circle using his Austrian citizenship to race one of the then fresh Cisitalias in Germany and elsewhere, though even he can't explain how he got that big frame into such a cramped car. He won the first post-war German race on Hockenheim Ring, finished second in Berne in 1948 and had a general run of success despite his age. Stuck also had a new project—the AFM built in his Garmisch garage.

This 2-litre monoposto was designed by Alex von Falkenhausen

Back to the circuits.
Winning his Autodrome G.P. heat in the AFM in 1950

around a much-altered BMW 328 engine (it later had its own power unit) and was at times prodigiously fast but overly prone to devour crankshafts after any great race distance.

'So we ran it mostly in hill-climbs,' Stuck recalls with that wide grin. For Hans it was the Austro-Daimler saga all over again. He had the old talent and one of the fastest cars but couldn't extract much more than a sprint from it, though his AFM did once lap Grenzlandring at 139 m.p.h. And on one lucky occasion he beat the 2-litre Veritas and Ferrari monopostos.

In 1953, in part for old times' sake, Stuck drove the four-camshaft Porsche Spyder in its first competitive events. But this was not a happy combination and he didn't find true winning form despite some Brazilian success. Stuck then sold fancy cars and used cars for a time and it was said the old mountain master was through at last—hardly surprising in his middle fifties.

But in this everybody reckoned without the Stuck amalgam of persistence and precision. He joined BMW in Munich and proved that the beautiful but overweight and somewhat unwieldy Type 507 V-8 coupé could beat a Ferrari 250 GT up a rainy hill—if Hans Stuck was driving. German Ferrari drivers still mutter at the memory. When BMW shifted their works competition interest to the tiny 700-c.c. Sport Coupé, Hans made concentration overcome a relative lack of power in his last German Mountain Campaign at the age of 60. More often than not in that season he was faster than the 1,000- and 1,300-c.c. cars two classes above him too.

This genial giant started racing with a backwards victory at 24 and passed his sixtieth birthday still winning. He had broken most of the bones in his body along the way and ignored an 'ivory elbow' but the easy smile was never vanquished. He lives now in the Bavarian Alps, still skis like an instructor and nurses a new driving talent named Stuck, a teen-age son who can already lap Nürburgring in competitive club times.

But then the boy learned from decades of dedicated application, funnelled into one man. Hans Stuck began with a win and retired still a champion; a motor boat and Grand Prix ace and all-time king of the mountains.

The principal racing successes of **HANS STUCK**

1931	1st:	Lwow G.P.
	2nd:	Masaryk G.P.
1934	1st:	German G.P.; Swiss G.P.; Masaryk G.P.
	2nd:	Italian G.P.; Eifelrennen
1935	1st:	Italian G.P.
	2nd:	German G.P.
1936	2nd:	German G.P.; Tripoli G.P.
	3rd:	Monaco G.P.; Swiss G.P.
1937	2nd:	Rio de Janeiro G.P.
1938	3rd:	German G.P.
1939	1st:	Bucharest G.P.
1948	2nd:	Prix de Berne.
1949	3rd:	Grenzlandring F. 2 Race.
1950	3rd:	Solitude G.P.
1951	1st:	Grenzlandring F.2 Race.

'Phi-Phi'

PHILLIPE ETANCELIN

by RODNEY WALKERLEY

BROAD-SHOULDERED, handsome, smiling, 'Phi-Phi' Etancelin was one of the great French drivers of the thirties who maintained the French racing tradition until the entire picture was changed in 1934 by the coming of the German teams to Grand Prix racing. Those were the great days of the battles between the 2·3-litre Bugatti and the mono-posto P.3 Alfa Romeo, and he was undoubtedly on equal terms with his compatriots—Louis Chiron, Marcel Lehoux, René Dreyfus and that Frenchman by adoption, Grover-Williams, who raced as 'Williams'. Their Italian antagonists were Tazio Nuvolari, Achille Varzi, Giuseppe Campari and Mario Borzacchini. With Louis Chiron, he was the only French veteran of that epoch to race again after the Hitler war, for Maurice Trintignant, Jean-Pierre Wimille and Raymond Sommer came to the starting grids several years later.

Etancelin was an independent and, like Sommer, drove always on the limit, matching his car against the factory entries and, like Sommer, he was a tiger. He drove, in blue overalls buttoned at neck and wrists and with a tweed cap worn back to front in the manner of the early days of motoring, crouched close to his wheel, elbows flashing up and down like pistons. Etancelin drove with great effort, in contrast to the calm, debonair Chiron, who delicately changed gear with thumb and two fingers and not gripping with his fist.

He drove with all courtesy. I cannot remember him involved with any other driver, nor, indeed, crashing his car. Thinking back to those splendid pre-war days, it seems that crashes were few and 'spinning off' even rarer, although the rigid, leaf-spring suspension, steering, road holding and brakes would appal a modern driver. He was, in style and even appearance, the kind of driver who handled the multi-litre four-cylinder monsters of the Gordon Bennett and the early Grands Prix, tough, fearless and dedicated to the proposition of pressing on, regardless, as fast as possible, in case something happened to interrupt his race.

As a man he was, at least in the racing milieu, easy to meet and ready to chat. As I remember, he spoke no English worth mentioning. He talked rapidly, eagerly and answered any question about his car and its performance without hesitation. And, once he had made your acquaintance he would come across a room or a crowded bar to shake your hand next time he saw you. I will swear that when he first put on a racing helmet—I think it was at Zandvoort for a Dutch Grand Prix soon after the war—his driving style changed. I have a note in my scribble-book of the time that 'the crash helmet instead of the tweed cap seems to have calmed Etancelin, who is driving as fast as ever and with the phlegm of his friend Louis Rosier'.

'Phi-Phi' came back to racing after the war in Ecurie France, the private team sponsored by a wealthy businessman, operating with the 4½-litre six-cylinder Talbots, built by Tony Lago. Etancelin found

Dieppe, 1934

these much to his liking for they were big cars in the immediate pre-war manner, in size and much larger than the 1½-litre Maseratis, Alfa Romeos and Ferraris against which they were raced; although the heavy Talbots lacked the power and the ultimate speed of the supercharged machines, their fuel consumption was twice as good (about 9 m.p.g.) and could run the usual 310-mile Grand Prix non-stop, a free gift of perhaps five minutes against the smaller cars that had to stop twice for fuel.

As a young man Etancelin's first mount was the ubiquitous Bugatti, probably the most successful racing and sports car ever marketed. (Ettore Bugatti made cars for sale, equally suitable for everyday sports-car use, or racing in Grand Prix and sports car events, for they were all two-seaters). It was with this model that he won the French Grand Prix of 1930, run outside Pau, and forced to ease up with petrol running lower and lower, was anxiously watching Henry Birkin's big Bentley closing on him fast in the last few miles. The following year he switched to Alfa Romeo and won three big races—Comminges, Dauphiné and Dieppe, where he drove four hours at 75 m.p.h.

By 1934 the P.3 2·9-litre Alfa Romeos of the Ferrari stable were supreme and Etancelin reverted to Bugatti for the lesser races and then acquired a Maserati, with which he won the Dieppe race again and took fourth place at Tripoli behind the Alfa Romeos. Motor racing was changing fast and there was now a diminishing role for the independent driver outside the groupings of the big teams. In 1936 he won the Pau Grand Prix again, now on the short, twisting circuit in the town, in the manner of the Monaco Grand Prix, and after that, unable to get a modern car for the new 3-litre/4½-litre Formula, he raced no more until the quasi-sports 4½-litre Talbot-Darracq took the field in 1938. These were ordinary two-seaters, stripped and tuned for racing and, of course, had not the slightest chance of even competing with the 3-litre supercharged Mercedes and Auto Unions.

However, a Frenchman first and last, Etancelin drove one of these cars in the Grand Prix of the Automobile Club of France at Rheims in July of 1938, backed by René Carrière, a Le Mans and rally driver. By any standards it was a curious affair, with the two French sports cars against Wimille's Bugatti, two Auto Unions with second-class drivers and three Mercedes driven by the champions Caracciola, von Brauchitsch and Lang, a total of nine cars if one includes the ineffective French S.E.F.A.C. which retired almost at once, out on the back of the circuit and was seen no more. Sensationally, both Auto Unions crashed on the opening lap, a measure of the inexperience of the drivers Christian Kautz and Rudolf Hasse. So, as the three Mercedes rushed on it was Etancelin who roared along in fourth place, while the Bugatti retired.

Etancelin and Carrière thereafter entertained the crowd and themselves in a private duel, in which, a length apart, Etancelin could not find the last few miles an hour to repass his friend, this being a circuit of long, full-throttle straights and not his metier at all. At last, on the one winding leg, with his car sideways most of the time and the tyres screaming, he got ahead by sheer speed of cornering on a two-mile stretch of curves. After about 115 miles, he blew up and that was that. It was a typical Etancelin drive, hopeless from the start but flat-out as long as the engine lasted. He got out of his car with a grin and a shrug to watch what was left of this fiasco of a race—three Mercedes chasing round and round with Carrière's Darracq 30 miles behind.

In 1949 when racing was once again in full international progress Phi-Phi joined the new Ecurie France. That year too, Juan Manuel Fangio arrived from Argentina to drive the little Simca-Fiat in Formula 2 races, and with it led Etancelin's Talbot single-seater into first place in the Marseilles Grand Prix. Then Etancelin won the Grand Prix of Paris at Montlhéry and ran second in the European Grand Prix at Monza and the Czech race at Brno. His hand had lost none of its cunning, but it was the day of the Type 158 $1\frac{1}{2}$-litre supercharged Alfa Romeo and although he drove with all his old fire the heavy Talbot, with perhaps 260 b.h.p., could not match the Italian cars, then driven by Fangio, Farina and Fagioli. We saw him at Silverstone in the International Trophy Race of 1951, unfamiliar in his safety helmet but still unmistakable as he hunched at his wheel and motored hard.

By 1951 the old Talbots were no longer winning races, even with Louis Rosier at the wheel, for now the V-12 $4\frac{1}{2}$-litre Ferrari was marching from success to success. Nevertheless, Etancelin took second place in the Grand Prix of the Netherlands and was third at Pescara. At the end of the year Alfa Romeos withdrew from racing for their $1\frac{1}{2}$-litre engine had reached the end of its potential and the financial situation ruled out the construction of a new car. That year Fangio became the World Champion.

Racing reverted to Formula 2 for the next two years, with Alberto Ascari world champion both seasons. Etancelin had no Formula 2 car. He brought the Talbot to Britain again in 1952 for a *formule libre* race at the Boreham circuit, where he finished third and then crossed to the Ulster Trophy on the Dundrod course, where he could do no better than fifth. After that he retired from racing.

In 1953 the Normandy Automobile Club ran their first event on the Rouen-les Essarts circuit and when the Rouenais Etancelin emerged from retirement with the Talbot again, to race on his own doorstep, he received an ovation from the crowd. Once again he drove the big

G.P. d'Europe, Silverstone, 1950

car as it should be driven, if in a somewhat less exuberant manner, for he was now 55 and grey-haired. It was his last race and his handling of the car was impeccable. That day he was a master again, handicapped by his obsolete car on an unsuitable, winding circuit where Farina and Mike Hawthorn on nimble 2-litre Ferraris were not only unbeatable but lapped everyone else.

In the closing stages Etancelin made his final effort. He thundered past a surprised Louis Rosier in another Ferrari and snatched third place. The applause at his finish was even more enthusiastic than for the winner. The veteran had completed his career in style, still a tiger. He raced no more. A new era dawned with the $2\frac{1}{2}$-litre Formula and the rise of new young drivers and new champions.

Rouen, 1953

The principal racing successes of **PHILIPPE ETANCELIN**

1926	3rd:	Coppa Florio.
1927	1st:	Marne G.P.
1929	1st:	La Baule G.P.; Comminges G.P.; Marne G.P.
1930	1st:	French G.P.; Dauphiné Circuit; Algerian G.P.
	3rd:	Lyons G.P.
1931	1st:	Comminges G.P.; Dauphiné Circuit; Dieppe G.P.
	2nd:	Casablanca G.P.
1932	1st:	Picardy G.P.
	2nd:	Casablanca G.P.
	3rd:	Tunis G.P.
1933	1st:	Marne G.P.; Picardy G.P.
	2nd:	French G.P.; Nimes G.P.
	3rd:	Pau G.P.

1934	1st:	Dieppe G.P.; Le Mans 24-hour Race.
	2nd:	Nice G.P.; Montreux G.P.; Casablanca G.P.
	3rd:	Vichy G.P.
1935	3rd:	Tunis G.P.
1936	1st:	Pau G.P.
1938	2nd:	Tourist Trophy
1939	3rd:	Pau G.P.
1949	2nd:	Italian G.P.
1951	2nd:	Dutch G.P.
	3rd:	Peruera G.P.
1952	3rd:	*Daily Mail* Trophy, Boreham.
1953	3rd:	Casablanca 12 hours; Rouen G.P.

JEAN-PIERRE WIMILLE

by EDWARD EVES

Monaco G.P., 1934

Winner at Le Mans, 1939

IT was somehow sadly appropriate that Jean-Pierre Wimille met death alone, driving a blue French car built in Paris. For, although born in the French capital, he lacked the usual gregarious nature of those born in great cities, and to most people seemed an aloof, lonely man.

The reason for his accident during practice for the 1949 Buenos Aires Grand Prix remains a mystery. Some say that J-P was dazzled by the low sun of that January morning, others that his scarf blew over his face. The most likely reason is that he tried to avoid a woman—Argentine spectators are notoriously unmanageable—who ran across the track in front of his car.

Certainly, his was not the case of a driver past his best who pulled out that last, fatal, stop. At the age of 41, Jean-Pierre, J-P as he was universally known, was at the peak of his ability. It had been a long peak admittedly, for his driving career had straddled the war, but only in the previous year he had been victor in the two premier races, the French and Italian Grands Prix, driving works 158 Alfa Romeos. He had also won the Rosario Grand Prix in the Argentine, the Grand Prix which was held to mark the re-opening of Monza, and many others. By coincidence, neither he nor his team-mate Count Carlo Felice Trossi, who was second in that Monza race, were to survive 1949, for Trossi died late in that year from a cancer which had overshadowed his life for years.

Alfa Romeo had been invincible in the great classic races of 1948, but the Type 158 was at the limit of its development, unbeaten but obsolete, and faced with a mounting challenge. For this reason, and because the engineering department desperately needed drawing office time on bread-and-butter cars, the pundits of Via Triaino decided to withdraw from racing, and Wimille was left without a car.

At about this time he had his own thoughts of retirement. He had designed and built a car in conjunction with a French engineer and he definitely intended to go into the manufacturing business. Possibly an association with Simca in the car project prompted him to choose the Formula 2 Simca-Gordini as his mount for the 1949 season, instead of the supercharged 1·5-litre Ferrari. He almost certainly knew of Alfa Romeo plans to come back in 1950 with the 159 and perhaps decided to take a breather in 1949 with Formula 2. Possibly his choice was conditioned by the fact that he had won the Rosario Grand Prix in a 1,220-c.c. Simca the previous year, and hoped to repeat the performance at Buenos Aires with the 1,430-c.c. model in 1949. The little Simca-Gordini was also a portent of things to come—lightweight and agile, it achieved fast circuit speeds by virtue of high speed through corners, rather than accelerative performance out of them.

Certainly his presence in the Argentine had made a lasting impression on one driver. As the greatest European driver of the day—this tends to be forgotten in the aura of the memories of more showy personalities

H

—J-P was the model on which a coming local driver, Juan Manuel Fangio, fashioned his driving technique. At a time when drivers worked in open cockpits, urging their cars round the circuits with brave flourishes of the wheel, Wimille in his neat French overalls sat back in the cockpit with his body motionless, only his arms and wrists working, complete master of any car. His style influenced Fangio and he had the same ideals of extreme physical fitness, probably because he was really not very strong. In all his modest way of life and his religious ideals may well have been responsible for the reputation for coldness which he gained among the high-living aces of the period.

Born in 1906, the son of a journalist, J-P jumped into motor racing at the deep end, entering a 2·3-litre Type 35 Bugatti in the Italian Grand Prix of 1931, sharing the driving with Jean Gaupillat. Organized by Vincenzo Florio at Monza, this rather boring ten-hour race was a runaway win for the new eight-cylinder Monza Alfa Romeo of Campari and Nuvolari. Persistent driving on the part of Wimille brought the two young *Bugattisti* home in fourth place, admittedly 100 miles behind the winner, but not very far behind such great men as Minoia and Borzacchini (Alfa Romeo) and Divo and Bouriat (Bugatti).

Obviously the Wimille family were wealthy, or young J-P had found a rich sponsor, for he was able to enter one of the latest twin camshaft 2·3 Type 51 Bugattis for the French Grand Prix at Montlhéry in the same year, unfortunately retiring with a broken radius rod. His first win came in the following year, at Oran in North Africa. On this African expedition he also drove one of the disappointing 4·9-litre Type 54 Bugattis at Tunis, and a 2·3 at Casablanca, retiring when in the lead at half-distance. The 4·9-litre car was no faster than the 2·3 Type 51, the brakes had difficulty in coping with the extra weight, and handling was poor, so not surprisingly it did not finish its particular race.

Late in 1932 he managed to acquire one of the 2·3-litre Monza Alfa Romeos, and with it won the Grand Prix de Lorraine at Nancy; at Comminges, he took the race lead after René Dreyfus in a Bugatti had crashed, only to do the same thing himself, rolling the Alfa and letting Zehender's Maserati into the lead.

Not until 1933 did Wimille begin to balance dash with judgement. His crashes the previous year and a lurid exhibition in the 1931 Belgian Grand Prix had earned him a reputation for wildness. His friend Marcel Lehoux, with whom he was often in competition and who he just beat in a number of minor Grands Prix, had been very critical of his driving methods during the 1932 season. But in his third year, still driving the faithful light blue and red Monza Alfa, he matured and he took second places at Comminges and in the Grand Prix de la Marne, to Fagioli's 2·65-litre Monoposto Alfa and Etancelin's Alfa Romeo respectively.

The first year of the 750-kg. formula, 1934, brought both satisfaction and disappointment. Satisfaction at being chosen for the Bugatti works team, with the possibility of driving the new 3·3-litre Type 59, and then disappointment with the car's performance. At Monaco, complete brake failure caused his retirement; in the French Grand Prix at Montlhéry he was able to demonstrate his powers of persistence by taking over Nuvolari's sick 3·3 and keeping it going for seventeen laps until it finally expired with selector trouble and severe misfiring. The 2900/8C Type B Alfa Romeos of Chiron, Varzi and Trossi-Moll were the only cars to run the full distance—only Benoist of the Bugatti team had phuttered through thirty-six laps, nearly to the finish—and there was no Bugatti entry in the German Grand Prix, while the works cars were given to Dreyfus, Benoist and Brivio for the Belgian G.P.

Only Dreyfus was given a works car for the first Swiss Grand Prix and there were no works cars for the Italian Grand Prix, either. At San Sebastian, however, in the Spanish Grand Prix, Wimille held second place for a time, splitting the Mercedes procession until carburetter trouble set him back to sixth place. His only win that year was at Algiers, where with no German opposition he was able to provide a victory for Bugatti, beating Chiron's 2·9 Alfa Romeo and Sofietti's Maserati in a straight fight.

The following year was more fruitful as the Type 59 was faster and reliable and J-P gained a second place to Achille Varzi's Auto Union at Tunis, a second to Chiron at Nancy and was fourth behind the Mercedes of Caracciola, Fagioli and von Brauchitsch in the Spanish Grand Prix at San Sebastian.

Bugatti decided to give up full-scale Grand Prix participation in 1936, but Wimille was sent out to South Africa with a Type 59 and was second to Massacurati's 2·3-litre car on handicap. From there he went to his favourite hunting ground, North Africa, for the Tunis race, following Caracciola's Mercedes and Pintacuda's Alfa Romeo home. Then there was a win in the Deauville Grand Prix and a trip to America for the Vanderbilt Cup race with a 4·7-litre single-seater Bugatti, in which he came second to Nuvolari's V-12 Alfa Romeo.

Again, in 1937 the classic French races were run for sports cars, a field in which there was no nasty foreign competition. Thus Wimille was able to win the Marne, Pau and Bône Grands Prix with the 3·3-litre sports Bugatti, and with Robert Benoist triumphed in the Le Mans 24-Hour Race.

There was a return to Grand Prix racing with a 3-litre engine installed in the 4·7-litre Bugatti chassis in 1938, but a piston burned out in the Cork Grand Prix, and an oil pipe broke after one lap in the French Grand Prix: Wimille's loyalty to, and patience with, Molsheim finally

Winner of the French G.P. in 1936 (Montlhéry)

. . . and 1948 (Rheims)

107

ran out at this, and he joined the Ferrari-run Alfa Romeo team for the Coppa Ciano race at Leghorn and the Swiss Grand Prix. In the former event he was stricken with a recurrent kidney trouble and Biondetti took over, finishing the car third behind Lang's Mercedes and Farina's Alfa. Turning down an offer to drive for Mercedes in 1939, he rejoined Bugatti, and in the tense atmosphere of the impending conflict, scored successes in minor Grands Prix, winning the Coupe de Paris with the 4·7-litre single-seater, finishing second to Lebegue's Talbot-Darracq at Comminges with the streamlined sports car, and winning the Luxembourg Grand Prix. Again his greatest success was with Veyron, at Le Mans, winning this classic for the second time with the sports 3·3-litre.

During the war J-P served in *l'Armée de l'Air* until France fell. Then, in common with other French drivers, he joined the Resistance movement and finished the war in his beloved North Africa, acting as a liaison officer with Allied troops.

Just how highly Wimille was regarded as a driver was shown by the invitation to join the Alfa Romeo works team as soon as they started racing again in 1946. He was the only non-Italian driver to be so honoured. (And, of course, the Type 158 Alfas were so obviously going to be almost invincible that there was no shortage of applicants).

By that time J-P had already been back in racing for more than a year, having won the first post-war race to be held in Europe, the Grand Prix de la Liberation held in the Bois de Boulogne, Paris, in September 1945. For this outing he brought out the streamlined 4·7-litre single-seater Bugatti which he had last driven at Prescott six years and one month previously. (And after it endowed Maurice Trintignant with his nickname *Petoulet*, by reason of Trint's retirement through a fuel blockage caused by rat droppings in the petrol tank of his Bugatti.)

The real revival of motor racing started in 1946, although there was no Formula except a free one. Numerous old Bugattis, Alfa-Romeos, Maseratis and what-have-you were unearthed from beneath strawstacks and inside barns all over France. It was also obvious that a lot of development had gone on in Italy, and new cars were available to the chosen few. There was a motor race somewhere in France most week-ends, and Wimille proceeded to win as many of them as possible in a pre-war 3-litre, eight-cylinder Alfa Romeo, adding the May Bois de Boulogne Grand Prix, the Perpignan Grand Prix, and the Grand Prix de Bourgogne to his score before joining Alfa Romeo for the Prix des Nations at Geneva.

This first real post-war Grand Prix, real in the sense that factory teams were taking part (as well as a heterogeneous selection of pre-war British-owned machinery). Farina, Wimille, Trossi and Varzi were the official Alfa Romeo works drivers. Wimille won his heat in the rain but was outclassed by Farina in the final. His temper was provoked on this occasion by a skid on a patch of oil which he attributed to Nuvolari nudging the tail of his car. Since the accident happened immediately after he had cut up the *Mantovane Volante* going into the self-same corner, he probably deserved what he got, and witnesses stated that Tazio was not to blame anyway. Nevertheless he restarted a stalled engine and finished in third place. He went on to win the Paris Grand Prix, again in the Bois de Boulogne, in the old 3-litre car, and to finish second to Achille Varzi in the Circuit of Turin, both driving 158 Alfas.

It was in this year that he had thoughts of going into the business

The blue of France again (Simca-Gordini, Lausanne, 1948

of motor manufacture. In collaboration with a Monsieur Viel, he had built a very *avant-garde*, three-seater, mid-engined coupé with aerodynamic body lines which would not look out of place today. It had a V-8 engine and rather unexpectedly, the Cotal electric gearbox was in front of the engine, and step-down gears were needed to lower the drive-line to take it under the engine to the final drive. The consequent high centre of gravity aft must have been something of an embarrassment when all-round independent suspension, with which the car was endowed, was still imperfectly understood . . .

Wimille's pre-occupation with motor manufacture did not keep him away from motor racing in 1947. Again he figured in the results of the major Grands Prix, first at Berne and first at Spa with the 158 Alfa, second to Villoresi's Maserati at Nice with an 1,100-c.c. Simca-Gordini.

Wimille's last full Grand Prix season was in the nature of a swan song. Farina had gone over to Maserati at Modena, and J-P was virtually cock-of-the-walk at Milan. With a choice of cars, he won the Italian, French and Monza Grands Prix and was second to his teammate Trossi in the Swiss race. In the 1,220-c.c. Simca-Gordini he won the Rosario Grand Prix, and drove his old 3-litre Alfa Romeo into third place in the Mar de Plata race. At Pau and Monaco he led both races in the Simca until it blew up, but was consoled by a second place, to Villoresi's Maserati, at Lausanne. Monza saw an Alfa walk-over, Wimille, Trossi, Sanesi and Taruffi finishing in that order, all in Tipo 158 cars. It was Wimille's last race.

Many experts regarded Wimille as the greatest driver of them all. Certainly he can be regarded as a link between the heroic age of driving and the modern style. For he had driven against Minoia, a veteran of the Edwardian era, in his first race, and in his final year had inspired Fangio's style, which influences drivers to this day.

The principal racing successes of **JEAN-PIERRE WIMILLE**

1932	1st:	Lorraine G.P.; Oran G.P.
1933	2nd:	Comminges G.P.; Marne G.P.
	3rd:	Masaryk G.P.
1934	1st:	Algerian G.P.
1935	2nd:	Tunis G.P.
	3rd:	Dieppe G.P.; Lorraine G.P.
1936	1st:	French G.P.; Comminges G.P.; Deauville G.P.
	2nd:	South African G.P.; G. Vanderbilt Cup.
	3rd:	Tunis G.P.
1937	1st:	Le Mans 24-hour Race; Marne G.P.; Pau G.P.; Bone G.P.
1938	3rd:	Coppa Ciano.
1939	1st:	Le Mans 24-hour Race; Coupe de Paris; Luxembourg G.P.
	2nd:	Comminges G.P.
1945	1st:	Coupe des Prisonniers.
1946	1st:	Burgundy G.P.; Coupe de Paris; Perpignan G.P.
	2nd:	Valentino G.P.
	3rd:	G.P. des Nations, Geneva.
1947	1st:	Belgian G.P.; Swiss G.P.; Coupe de Paris; R. Benoist Cup.
	2nd:	Nice G.P.; Lausanne G.P.
	3rd:	Lyons G.P.
1948	1st:	French G.P.; Italian G.P.; Autodrome G.P.; Monza; Valentino G.P.; Rosario G.P.
	2nd:	Swiss G.P.
	3rd:	Mar del Plata G.P.

Mechanics' attitudes to a driver are usually revealing . . . (Tripoli in 1937—a photograph taken by Nuvolari)

RAYMOND SOMMER

by JOHN EASON GIBSON

IN the maelstrom of activity common in racing circles today, where the drivers' world tends to be bounded by airports, motels and frantic rushes from circuit to circuit the world over, there seems to be little time to remember the drivers of even the immediate past. There are, no doubt, many enthusiastic and knowledgeable followers of the sport who, as well as having no knowledge of the great days in the middle 'thirties, know but little—or have forgotten what they knew—of the exciting days during the first fifteen years of the post-war period. Those young followers of the sport who know only the sometimes over-dedicated, and on occasion perhaps over-commercial, drivers of today have missed much.

In an odd way it is often the paying spectators rather than those who are more intimately involved in the sport who pick the most admirable drivers. It was the public who first decided that drivers like Nuvolari, Hawthorn, Scott Brown and Sommer were their idea of the racing driver and this opinion was probably based on the very obvious enjoyment drivers like them got from their racing. Even to those who had never met him, Sommer in many ways typified their own romantic idea of what the racing driver should be: gay, debonair and casual out of the car; dour, pugnacious and a fierce fighter once the flag fell.

Sommer's whole career was coloured by the difference in his early background from that of the average professional driver of his time. One of three sons of the wealthy French felt manufacturer Roger Sommer, himself a wildly enthusiastic aviator in his younger days, Raymond started his racing on rather similar lines to the rich young amateurs who were the backbone of British racing in the early thirties. But very soon his pride dictated that if some others were considered to be worth large sums of starting money, so too was Sommer. From then on he was the complete professional, even if only as far as his relations with race organizers were concerned.

Most of those who remember Sommer will think first of his driving since the Second World War, but his pre-1939 experience included such varied cars as Alfa Romeo and Chrysler at Le Mans, the 2·9-litre Maserati and Monoposto Alfa Romeo in the major Grands Prix and the Type 158 Alfa Romeo just before mobilization. Twice he won at Le Mans, partnered in 1932 by Chinetti (although Sommer drove for all but three of the twenty-four hours) and then in 1933 with Nuvolari, from whom much of Raymond's philosophy of racing was learned and for whom he had an almost schoolboy's admiration. Having the advantage of financial independence, which prevented him from regarding money as the motive for any action, he developed a very individual attitude to racing. Accepting a place in a factory team merely for financial security never appealed, nor did the consequent benefit of almost certain victory. For him the whole point of motor racing was the battle

Champion of unproved causes. During practice with the C.T.A.-Arsenal at Lyon, 1947

111

and the greatest attraction in post-war years lay in trying to split the pre-arranged finishing order of the Alfa Romeo team with a rather breathless Maserati from Scuderia Milan, or in trying to beat the almost supreme Ferrari with his own out-dated and ponderous Talbot. The number of times he succeeded in upsetting the forecasts of complacent team managers is an indication of how hard he fought.

In common with some other drivers, Sommer kept a most complete personal diary in which every detail of his racing was noted. His time from home to the circuit—always by road—or from circuit to circuit; details of the best hotels and restaurants; voltage for the electric razor; a frank and honest report of both training and the race; and, by far the most important, his own personal score card for every race. At the end of each season Raymond audited his personal score, and the important thing was that the highest scores were given to the races in which he had fought well and never did any easy win over slight opposition merit the full ten marks. The cliché born in the Bentley days that 'you cannot finish unless you stay on the road and you cannot win unless you finish' was rather secondary to Sommer. He believed strongly that the idea was to see who could go fastest. Because of that and because he was usually fighting factory teams with superior equipment, he was most impressed with his fastest laps and the number of times he had held the lead.

While more than capable of holding his own in the most ruthless cut-and-thrust of Grand Prix racing, his manners on the circuit to lesser mortals and to beginners were perfect. I can remember him many times devoting much of the training period at Continental races to showing aspiring British drivers the way round. His helpfulness went further. In the difficult days of currency restrictions in post-war Europe no British driver needed to look further than Sommer when there was any danger of the wolf breaking down the garage door; to those he knew well such help was generously given without the asking.

In that hectic year of 1947 he succeeded in splitting the Alfa Romeo team at Berne in the Swiss Grand Prix. After ten laps of the final had been covered he was leading Trossi and Sanesi by 45 seconds with Wimille and Varzi in front. While Trossi got through during Sommer's pit stop, caused by the unreasonable thirst of the Scuderia Milan Maserati, he held off the new man Sanesi. A day's work good enough to please the Maserati fans and depress the good Guidotti's confidence more than somewhat. During the race at Berne, Wimille's fastest lap when winning was 96·85 m.p.h., while Sommer's was 97·03 m.p.h.; not much in it, but proof that he was trying rather than accepting a safe place behind the Alfas.

Earlier the same year he had a satisfying drive at Lausanne with an 1,100 Simca-Gordini against 'B. Bira' in an identical car. Despite Bira's weight advantage—probably 8½ stone against 15 stone—there was nothing in it, and the Siamese driver won by only one car's length, but during the race Raymond had to do almost a complete lap carrying a trailing exhaust pipe after a bracket had broken. As he himself explained after the race—'*La voiture etait un peu lourde! alors j'enléve le tube d'échappement pendant la course, car "le poids ç'est l'ennemi".*'

It is indicative that many discerning journalists christened him Raymond Coeur de Lion—a particularly apt *nom de volant*—and a study of some of his races will prove its justification. In the Grand Prix of Belgium at Spa-Francorchamps in 1950 he was faced with a

Nearing the end of a 21-hour drive. Le Mans, 1932

The exhaust incident at Lausanne, 1947

Swiss G.P., 1950

team of three Alfa Romeos led by Fangio and two Ferraris in the hands of Ascari and Villoresi; opposition which would tempt most drivers, especially at the wheel of a lorry-like Talbot, to motor round for a nice safe place. But this was never Raymond's way. Right from the start he drove as hard as the Talbot would go. First he attacked Ascari and took over fifth place, then Villoresi was taken on that frightening imitation straight between Malmedy Corner and Stallebras Curve, but instead of being content with a safe fourth place behind the 'unbeatable' Alfas he kept on at them. Justification came when the three red cars stopped to replenish and into the lead sailed the interloper to gain a lead of 25 seconds before they returned to the battle. Although the three Alfas repassed him and he then went out with the almost inevitable Talbot engine trouble, he had justified himself by really going racing and by leading the combined might of Alfa and Ferrari. He gave himself 9 out of 10 marks for that race, although his notes show that a tyre change on the right front would have been needed before the full distance could have been covered. It is worth remembering that his average speed when in the lead was 110·41 m.p.h. against Fangio's winning average of 109·77 m.p.h. He must have enjoyed leading the Alfas, as it was at St. Cloud in 1946 that he had truly beaten them.

His catholic tastes are shown by the makes he drove during his career; Chrysler, Ratier, Hotchkiss, Alfa Romeo, Maserati, Talbot, Cisitalia, Simca, BMW, CTA-Arsenal, OSCA, Bugatti, B.R.M., Ferrari, H.W.M. and Aston Martin. His private cars were equally well chosen: Lancia Aprilia, BMW 335 and a Mk. VI Bentley. Every run in every car was regarded as a training run, with average speeds and delays at frontiers carefully jotted in the diary. One year at Silverstone he drove both a Cooper and an Aston Martin—the year his B.R.M. broke the

Relaxed in a Talbot (Swiss G.P., 1949)

transmission on the line—and on hearing that Lance Macklin could not drive the H.W.M. because of a poisoned thumb he rushed round to try and get a drive on that; just like an enthusiastic beginner at his first race meeting.

It was, somehow, in character that Raymond should have met his death at the wheel of a little Cooper, into which he had fitted a 1,100-c.c. twin-cylinder engine, and which he was driving 'for the hell of it' in a minor French event. His own character is probably demonstrated best by his frank comments on other drivers when asked by inquisitive journalists. He never based his opinions on the drivers' known successes but rather on his ability to fight. When sometimes he could not come up with an answer he explained his inability: 'It is impossible to say, I have never battled with him.'

The principal racing successes of **RAYMOND SOMMER**

1928	2nd:	Antibes G.P.	1945	2nd:	Coupe des Prisonniers.
1932	1st:	Le Mans 24-hour Race; Marseilles G.P.	1946	1st:	Coupe du Salon, Montlhéry; Forez G.P.; Lille F.1. Race; Marseilles G.P.; St. Cloud G.P.
	2nd:	Nice Circuit.			
	3rd:	Comminges G.P.		2nd:	Nice G.P.
1933	1st:	Le Mans 24-hour Race.		3rd:	Brussels Sports Car Race; Marseilles Sports Car Race; Valentino G.P.
	2nd:	Picardy G.P.; Spa 24-hour Race.	1947	1st:	Valentino G.P.
	3rd:	Marne G.P.		2nd:	Albi G.P.; Circuit des Remparts, Angoulême; R. Benoist Cup; Prix de Leman.
1934	2nd:	Belgian G.P.; Picardy G.P.			
1935	1st:	G.P. de France; Comminges G.P.	1948	1st:	Coupe des Petites Cylindrées, Rheims; Florence F.2. Race; Geneva Voiturette G.P.
	3rd:	Marne G.P.; Picardy G.P.		3rd:	Italian G.P.; G.P. des Nations, Geneva.
1936	1st:	French G.P.; Spa 24-hour Race.	1949	1st:	Coupe du Salon, Montlhéry; Prix de Leman.
1937	1st:	Marseilles G.P.; Tunis G.P.		3rd:	Swiss G.P.
	2nd:	Pau G.P.	1950	1st:	Aix les Bains F.2. Race; G.P. du Nord; Prix de Berne.
1939	1st:	Circuit des Remparts, Angoulême;			
	2nd:	Antwerp G.P.; Coupe de Paris.		2nd:	Monza Sports Car Race.
	3rd:	Comminges G.P.		3rd:	Medoc F.2. Race.

Nürburgring, 1938

DICK SEAMAN

by WILLIAM BODDY

BORN on February 4, 1913, in Sussex, the son of very wealthy parents, Richard John Beattie-Seaman can be said to have bridged the gap between the rich amateur racing driver and the professionals of later years.

Educated at Rugby and Trinity College, Cambridge, Dick Seaman spent much of his summer holidays in France and when in this country divided his spare time between his father's London house in Ennismore Gardens and their country place, first Kentwell Hall in Suffolk, a moated house standing in a 5,000-acre estate, and later at Weald Hall in Essex, an Elizabethan house with a lake, a deer park and some fine shooting.

In other words, the young Seaman was brought up to enjoy and expect the privileges which wealthy parents of those days could and did provide for their children. He first turned to motoring sport merely as an extension of other outdoor pursuits, although from an early age he had tended to look upon the motor-car—his father owned an Edwardian Daimler and Dick was taught to drive at Weald Hall by the chauffeur, while still at his prep. school—as likely to have a profound influence on his later life.

Before going up to Cambridge, Seaman took part in a number of reliability trials with a Riley and entered the car for a Shelsley Walsh hill-climb in 1931. It is perhaps significant, in view of his later very close association with the American millionaire Whitney Straight, that Seaman was second in his class, which was won by Straight, who was also driving a Riley. At Cambridge he met Straight, continued to drive in reliability trials with an M.G. Magna, and did some rowing. Ignoring the social life of the University, Seaman concentrated on widening his experience of motoring sport, driving his M.G. in the strenuous Alpine Trial and then acquiring from Papworth a 2-litre un-supercharged Grand Prix Bugatti, which he raced at Brooklands and Donington.

Up to now Seaman represented the keen British amateur racing motorist. In this world, Brooklands brought together a remarkable collection of racing cars of different ages and types, racing on a handicap basis in an atmosphere of sartorial elegance and garden party surroundings, while at Donington a dilettante form of road racing had just commenced.

It wasn't long before Richard Seaman looked for more serious outlets for his driving prowess and mechanical aptitude. Whitney Straight, almost alone among enthusiasts in this country, had realized that motor racing could be run on a business basis without detracting from the sport and excitement that it provided. He had achieved considerable success at home and on the Continent with an M.G. Magnette and a 2·5-litre Maserati; by 1933 he decided to make motor racing his profession and Seaman, by now a close friend, was enthralled. Straight had his own light plane at Cambridge in which he flew to race meetings.

'. . . a rather self-conscious salute . . .'

(Seaman was taught to fly at Heston and later acquired a Gipsy Moth of his own and was later to show outstanding ability as a private pilot by flying out to the Monaco G.P. in bad weather conditions.)

Buying an ex-Straight M.G. Magnette, Seaman turned his back on Cambridge after the Lent term of 1934. He was to devote his future exclusively to professional motor racing, a great blow to his parents, who had recently bought him a 2-litre Lagonda and had hoped that he would return to their new country place, Pull Court, near Tewkesbury, and that he would train for a diplomatic, legal or parliamentary career.

But Dick's mind was made up and from then on he put all his energies into becoming better and better known as a racing driver, and to becoming a front-rank racing driver. He spent a great deal of time writing letters from his office at Ennismore Gardens and quite ruthlessly extracted as much free service and free materials from the Trade as possible. His career with the M.G. went well. After winning his class at the Inter-'Varsity Speed Trials, but having little success at Brooklands, the M.G. was placed third in the small car race at Pescara, behind two similar M.Gs., won the Prix de Berne, and before the 1934 season was over Seaman had come in fifth in the Masaryk G.P. in Czechoslovakia and second in the Nuffield Trophy Race at Donington Park. This was run over a slippery course and something of Seaman's skill as a racing driver had been seen by the discerning amongst the English race-goers who attended these meetings.

Seaman's next move was to borrow a works K3 M.G. Magnette on a business footing for the East London G.P. in South Africa, immediately after Christmas. He and Straight flew out from Heston in a de Havilland Dragon—this is somehow typical of that golden age of motor racing— Straight won the race in a Maserati; Seaman finished fifth.

After this Whitney Straight dropped racing in favour of a career offering greater financial security and Seaman was obliged to carry on alone. This he did with characteristic determination. Having persuaded his mother to buy him one of the new 1½-litre E.R.A.s, which he finished in his colours of black with silver wheels, Seaman acquired a Dodge van in which to transport it and entered into an agreement with E.R.A. Ltd. as to how his car was to be entered and prepared. His initial appearance as an E.R.A. driver was at a Donington Club meeting but in a works E.R.A., as his own was not ready. He finished second in his first race behind Charlie Martin's 2·3-litre Bugatti, having been hampered by brake and other mechanical troubles.

The young British driver was determined to compete in as many Continental *Voiturette* races as possible and was negotiating with the organizers about starting money. His own black E.R.A. did not materialize for a long time and it was not until June 1935 that he was able to race abroad, in the G.P. des Frontieres at Chimay. The E.R.A. developed trouble and Seaman retired—indeed it soon became apparent that his skill could not compensate for this car's refusals to function properly.

At the Eifelrennen race in Germany Seaman got his E.R.A. in front of the works E.R.A.s and the Maseratis but it was losing oil and this dropped him back so that he eventually finished fourth, behind Mays, Ruesch and Rose-Richards; at the Kesselberg hill-climb brake trouble ruined his chances. Back to England for the Nuffield Trophy race, the E.R.A. was so unsatisfactory that Seaman was obliged to withdraw.

He went to Dieppe and pressed Mays's works E.R.A. mercilessly, until once again trouble caused him to retire.

Clearly, Seaman had to do something drastic to rectify these poor performances. He declared that as the E.R.A. factory at Bourne was so busy with other cars, he would attend to the E.R.A. himself. At the same time he gave up his aeroplane in favour of a Ford V-8 for travel to and from the circuit. Setting up a garage behind the house in London, he appointed Jock Finlayson as his racing mechanic, and Tony Birch as his manager.

This new arrangement was immediately successful. During the latter part of the 1935 season the black E.R.A. won its class and made second fastest time in the Grossglockner hill-climb, won easily at Pescara at 78·9 m.p.h., had another easy victory at Berne, at 82·64 m.p.h., repeated its Grossglockner showing at Freiburg and won comfortably at Brno, averaging 81·4 m.p.h. to complete the E.R.A. hat-trick. Beating the best of the works E.R.A.s with no holds barred, in hill-climbs as well as races, must have seemed like poetic justice to Seaman after his poor beginning to the season. He also drove an M.G. into tenth place in the T.T. and proved no coward when it came to driving the difficult Duesenberg round the Brooklands outer circuit, for sharing this American single-seater with Featherstonhaugh, who still drives fast cars fast, the pair kept going for seventy-two laps of the race.

There followed one of the most remarkable achievements in the annals of British motor racing history. Seaman was faced with the prospect of using the E.R.A. again in 1936 or looking for a new car. Persuaded by Giulio Ramponi, he acquired from Earl Howe one of the complicated straight-eight 1½-litre Delage cars designed some eleven years earlier by Lory. These low-built supercharged cars had swept all before them in their day but were now regarded as heavy, crudely braked and rather past it. But, working in his small garage in Ennismore Gardens mews, Seaman put all his ability into having the old car rebuilt in lighter, more powerful form. Writing letters without end to

With the black Delage, Pescara, 1936

all manner of suppliers, Dick Seaman obtained the most favourable terms for materials and components when he couldn't obtain them for nothing, negotiated starting money terms, talked bonus money with the petrol, oil and accessories firms and generally embarked on a one-man professional motor racing career.

Given Lockheed hydraulic brakes, its engine painstakingly tuned by Ramponi and the weight lopped off the chassis and body, Seaman set his Delage, which today would be regarded as a vintage car, to attack the best $1\frac{1}{2}$-litre cars that E.R.A., Maserati and the rest could field. It worked! But only because Seaman had emerged as an impeccable driver, never wasting a fraction of a second or over-stressing his car, and because he was able to run through a long race without refuelling the comparatively lightly supercharged engine of the once-World-Champion Delage. He borrowed a 3-litre Maserati from Harry Rose for the B.R.D.C. Empire Trophy Race at Donington and attended to the delicate task of linering down its engine to just under 2,700 c.c. to suit the class handicap system. This enabled Seaman to beat Fairfield's E.R.A., his spirited drive winning the race at 66·3 m.p.h. But his heart was with the rebuilt black Delage. After trying it out at a small Donington meeting and winning two races, Seaman took his car over to the Isle of Man and won the R.A.C. Light Car Race at 69·76 m.p.h., once again vanquishing the E.R.A.s. That the Delage did not exactly run away from the modern opposition was apparent at Nürburg and again at Péronne, for in both cases Seaman drove too ambitiously and crashed. But he was on form again at Pescara, winning at 77·1 m.p.h. from the Maserati opposition. After this the combination of the calm calculating Seaman and the reliable rejuvenated Delage proved invincible. Meeting the works E.R.A. team and the privately-entered Maserati contingent at Berne, the 1927 Delage came home the victor at 87·86 m.p.h.

Seaman then returned to England and enthusiasts at home were able to see the gallant Delage win its third successive race, for although its engine had not been stripped between events, Seaman was able to humour it so that although Howe's E.R.A. took the lead in the J.C.C. 200-mile Race at Donington, he had to stop for fuel, enabling Seaman, just as in the I.o.M., to run non-stop and win, at 69·28 m.p.h. It was a magnificent end to a fantastic engineering gamble and put Seaman into the lead for the B.R.D.C. Gold Star, which he ultimately lost to Prince Bira by one point.

The fact is that Seaman's interest tailed off towards the close of the 1936 season, because neither Mercedes-Benz nor Alfa Romeo would lend him a suitable fast car in which to defend his Star points in the Brooklands Mountain Handicap. He was, however, turning his thoughts to driving big cars and, sharing a 3·8-litre Alfa Romeo with Ruesch, had won the Donington Grand Prix. Seaman had also driven a Maserati with Trossi unsuccessfully at the Nürburgring, shared the wheel of a $4\frac{1}{2}$-litre Lagonda in the Spa 24-hour race, and retired from the T.T. in which he started in a sports Aston Martin.

The quite remarkable aspect of Seaman's racing up to this point was his unshakeable determination, which enabled him to beat the finest factory-prepared British and Italian $1\frac{1}{2}$-litre cars with his outdated racing car rebuilt on a not very long shoestring in a small garage-workshop, and his driving ability. This was so outstanding that it brought an invitation to join the mighty Mercedes-Benz team, then

Big-car experience (Donington, 1936)

120

British works driver for Mercedes-Benz
(Donington, 1938)

racing the fastest and most powerful Grand Prix cars in the World, despite his limited 'big-car' experience and the fact that his victories had been achieved only in *voiturette* class cars.

This summons to take tests to see if he qualified for the most exacting and dangerous racing of all changed Seaman's plans. His ideas for a single-seater-width light-alloy chassis for the Delage and his attempts to get Dr. Porsche to build him a car to take a couple of Napier Dagger aero-engines for an attempt on the Land Speed Record at Daytona were shelved. He had become a true professional. He sold the Delage and went to live in Germany, dedicated to driving for the Hitler-inspired Daimler-Benz racing organization.

This proved no easy road to fame. He had a very nasty accident while testing a 1936 Mercedes-Benz at Monza, wrecking the car and injuring one of his legs. Yet from the very first race in which he drove the German cars, Seaman did exceptionally well. By the end of the 1937 season Dick Seaman had experienced another serious crash, mechanical troubles had sometimes held him back or caused him to retire, but he was fifth in the Avusrennen, second in the American Vanderbilt Cup Race, fifth with Caracciola at Pescara, and fourth at Leghorn and Brno.

Through all this intensive racing Seaman remained boyish, unruffled, honest about his mistakes, proud to the point of simplicity when he did well; delighted in seeing his old friends when the team came to Donington Park, remembering those with whom he was but casually acquainted.

He was, in fact, a charming ambassador for his country, now so close to another World War.

Seaman faced the 1938 season with confidence, even if aware that his place in a German racing team was difficult in view of the precarious political situation. He married a German girl against his mother's wishes, and for Daimler-Benz won the German G.P., acknowledging this lifelong ambition with a rather self-conscious Nazi salute, came home second at Berne, and third at Donington. He was allowed to drive a 328 B.M.W. in the T.T.

By 1939 Seaman was troubled by the worsening situation but was reassured by Lord Howe that he was serving his country best by staying with the German team. Keeping fit by ski-ing, Seaman showed no outward concern in spite of his inner thoughts and after retiring from the Eifelrennen went to Spa for the Belgian G.P., delighted to be with English friends.

The race started in rain, and even the experienced Caracciola skidded off the road. Seaman was driving at the top of his form, closing on Muller's Auto Union, until, on the twenty-second lap, thirteen from the end, when he had taken the lead, with Lang behind him, he skidded at La Source, and his Mercedes-Benz went into the trees. The car caught fire and Seaman died from the injuries he received. The greatest British Grand Prix driver since Segrave was mourned by his countrymen and although Britain was on the brink of war with Germany, orders came from Berlin that Dick Seaman was to be buried with full honours; among the wreaths was one from Adolf Hitler . . .

Thus, tragically, died a young man, wealthy in his own right, who was dedicated to motor racing. In those days green cars were not even in evidence on the starting grids but our prestige was strengthened by the courage and skill Dick Seaman displayed driving in the most exciting and exacting road racing cars the world had ever seen.

The principal racing successes of **DICK SEAMAN**

1934	1st:	Prix de Berne.
	2nd:	Nuffield Trophy, Donington.
	3rd:	Pescara Voiturette Race.
1935	1st:	Masaryk Voiturette Race; Pescara Voiturette Race; Prix de Berne.
1936	1st:	Pescara Voiturette Race; Prix de Berne; Empire Trophy; J.C.C. 200; Donington G.P.; Douglas Light Car Race.
1937	2nd:	Vanderbilt Cup.
1938	1st:	German G.P.
	2nd:	Swiss G.P.
	3rd:	Donington G.P.

HERMANN LANG

by DAVID HODGES

Early victory—Avus, 1937

Late victory—Le Mans, 1952

WHENEVER the drivers of the two great pre-war German teams walked to their cars on the grids and the mechanics left them, the gulf separating the linen-helmeted heroes and their slightly less impeccable minions seemed enormous, yet one man, Hermann Lang, moved from one world to the other without apparently taking an intermediate step. As, in effect, a fledgeling driver, he finished fifth in his first-ever circuit race—driving a 430-b.h.p. Mercedes-Benz at the Nürburgring to boot —and within three seasons established himself as one of the tiny exclusive group who could really exploit the fabulous German machines of the era. Then in the last pre-war season of G.P. racing he won five of the seven races, seven of the ten events, in which he started, to become European Champion . . .

Hermann Lang was born on April 6, 1909, at Bad Cannstatt near Stuttgart. Like so many leading Grand Prix drivers he began his racing career as a motor cyclist, perhaps even more naturally than most as he served an apprenticeship as a mechanic in a motor cycle factory. He gained his first race victory on Stuttgart's local circuit, Solitude, riding a Norton shared with one of his brothers; by the late twenties he was a works rider for the Standard company and thereafter he concentrated on driving sidecar outfits, making his mark at least nationally as a hill-climb specialist. However, a racing department was a luxury which no manufacturer could afford in the depressed last years of the Weimar Republic, so that by the summer of 1932 Lang was pleased enough to find employment driving a diesel locomotive on an industrial light railway.

Indirectly through this very down-to-earth job, mischance and chance now coming in favourable sequence, Lang moved on to work for Daimler-Benz as a mechanic; moreover, he joined the staff of the test department where the M.25 engine was being developed for the 1934 750-kg. Grand Prix Formula. When that season opened he was transferred to Neubauer's racing department and throughout it travelled the circuits as Luigi Fagioli's mechanic. Towards its end, and not quite incidentally, he was entered in the German 2,000 km. Reliability Trial, gaining a Gold Medal and the further attention of the redoubtable Neubauer, who selected him to join a group of German aspirants in driver tests at Monza in the spring of 1935.

So without benefit of experience in a cadet class, and with the classic Neubauer imprecation 'If you run out of road, you may as well buy a train ticket home' as encouragement, Lang was let loose with a W.25, a car which he had previously driven from paddock to grid or in occasional tests of machinery. He passed these more personal tests with flying colours—certainly Neubauer was pleased and was to be increasingly pleased as the seasons passed until he came to regard Lang as one of the best drivers ever.

While remaining Fagioli's mechanic, he thus became 'driver under training', effectively the Number Five in the hierarchy of Mercedes drivers (Caracciola, Fagioli, and von Brauchitsch with Geier as official reserve). As fourth man, Geier drove in the first of the major 1935 events, the Avusrennen, and was stood down to allow Lang to gain race experience in the Eifelrennen. In practice and in the race, Lang contrived to run out of road! However, neither incident was serious and with the help of spectators or marshals he got going again to complete practice and to finish fifth in his first race. But his 540-degree race spin on the damp Nürburgring reinforced his mistrust of wet circuits; his inability to cope with such conditions remained his principal weakness for several seasons.

The following season was unhappy for Mercedes-Benz, for their cars won only twice, at Monaco and Tunis. In the spring, Lang (who had taken the injured Geier's place) again finished fifth in the Eifel-rennen—a performance unremarked when Rosemeyer drove an astonishing race in foul conditions. Back at the Ring for the German Grand Prix, he led for a lap, broke a finger changing gear and handed over to Caracciola, whose own car had broken down. But he was now beginning to show his inherent ability and inclination to 'tiger' and in turn he took over von Brauchitsch's car, so that although he finished only seventh he again attracted attention; when Neubauer (and hence Mercedes) and Fagioli explosively parted company, Lang became a full member of the team.

Native hills—Freiburg, 1937

The first two races of 1937 were very, very fast affairs. Lang won both. He liked this type of event in any case, but now in addition to the vital will to win and a sympathy for machinery—presumably inbred somewhere in his background as a mechanic—he demonstrated a mastery of race tactics. To a large extent the credit for these two victories is due to Lang's cool head for the tactics of the pre-war Mercedes teams were not always laid down so absolutely as it is sometimes re-called that they were. In the Tripoli G.P. on the Melhalla, he kept in touch with the leaders—a very select quartet comprising, at various times during the race, Caracciola, von Brauchitsch, Fagioli and Rose-meyer—conserved his tyres and made only his planned pit stop while they made additional tyre stops, and won at 134·25 m.p.h. In the final of the Avusrennen, where he drove a fully-streamlined W.125, he again judged precisely the strains which tyres and machinery would stand, this time winning at an average speed of 162·61 m.p.h. Curiously— for he had demonstrated that he had come completely to terms with 640-b.h.p. Grand Prix cars—he enjoyed no more outright victories in 1937, although he followed Caracciola across the line by a split second in the Italian and Swiss Grands Prix, and for him the season ended tragically in a serious accident in the Masaryk G.P. when his car rolled into a group of spectators.

In his first full season of racing, Hermann Lang thus almost fully equipped himself for the 1938–40 3-litre Formula; during its two effective years he was first to equal and then outshine Caracciola as its most outstanding driver.

On paper 1938 was little better for Lang than 1937; he won two races. But so did Nuvolari and Caracciola—nobody won more in front line racing—and Lang never finished lower than third while he was invariably on the front row of a grid.

The new season began inauspiciously enough when the W.154 which he shared with Caracciola at Pau was beaten into second place

Tripoli hat trick—bringing in the W.165, 1939

by Dreyfus's unsupercharged Delahaye. But the world was turned right way up again at Tripoli; this time Lang's tactic was to attack and drop the rest of the field. No mean target in itself, but he lapped every other runner to win at 127·45 m.p.h. (with an engine of only just over half the capacity of that in his 1937 car). Successively, he then finished third in the French G.P. (in effect a Mercedes walkover that year) raising the Rheims lap record by 4·1 m.p.h. and took over Caracciola's car to finish second to Seaman in the German G.P. His second victory of the year was also his first on a 'slow' circuit, at Leghorn in the Coppa Ciano.

And so to 1939. As the year opened there were apparently half a dozen fairly evenly matched top men driving the fairly evenly matched cars of two marques. At its premature end, Hermann Lang was undisputed European Champion and had gained the Hill Climb Championship on which his heart had been set since he started racing cars. In winter practice he had overcome his wet-road weakness, as ever he was physically fit and determined to win races, his methods in doing just this were to be quite straightforward and level-headed. Short, he sat well down in the Mercedes cockpit; nevertheless the outward impression is of powerful shoulders and arms. Heavy-footed thruster he may have been, but there was more to the man than this—so much at least is evident in his record in keeping cars on the road and in keeping them going.

Once again the season opened at Pau—Mercedes-Benz feeling morally obliged to run in this fairly minor event—but in 1939 the only challenge to Lang came from his team-mate, von Brauchitsch. In his third Tripoli G.P. Lang repeated his 1938 tactics (this time in Mercedes' W.165 'secret weapon') just as successfully, his winning speed with $1\frac{1}{2}$ litres being 122·9 m.p.h., although as the race ran out he was backing off so as not to lap Caracciola (despite a smouldering feud between the two men). For the rest of the year the team raced the superb W.163, moving from Melhalla's sweeping full-throttle curves to the

125

German Grand Prix, 1937 and . . .   *. . . 1954—his last Grand Prix*

sinuous Nürburgring for the Eifelrennen, another Lang race and the
one in which he set the 9 minutes 52 seconds lap record which was
to stand until 1956, when Fangio broke it with a 2·5 litre Lancia-
Ferrari.

Lang also put in the fastest lap at Spa (in a very wet race, be it noted)
but found little joy in winning this Belgian Grand Prix for he was more
upset by Seaman's accident than any other during his career. His own
triumphant progress was interrupted in the next two races, ironically
the two which he most wanted to win but never did: he led both in
their early stages but in complete contrast with the 1938 French G.P.
Rheims saw a complete Mercedes debacle in 1939, although this time
Lang pushed the lap record up by 9·7 m.p.h., and he also retired in the
German G.P. But in the Swiss Grand Prix he beat the *regenmeister*
Caracciola in the rain and in a straight fight, thus securing the Championship. Meanwhile he had gained the hill-climb title he coveted,
clinching it with a f.t.d. on the Grossglockner in rain *and* mist.

During the years of the Second World War, which should by all
indications have been his peak years as a driver, Lang inspected
Daimler-Benz aircraft components. He reappeared on the sporting
scene in the summer of 1946, gaining a hill-climb class win with a 2-
litre B.M.W. Thereafter he occasionally dabbled in motor sport until,
in 1950, he apparently saw some promise in the Formula 2 Veritas; as
far as he was concerned this promise was hardly fulfilled, for to offset
retirements at Bremgarten and the Nürburgring he was placed only
in a minor event at Solitude.

Then in 1951 he was able to race with his heart in the business again.
As a member of a Mercedes-Benz works team, driving W.163s,
moreover. These cars were run in two 97-mile races in Argentina and,
true to his tradition with them, Lang was on the front row of the grid

for each race—in pole position for the first. But the machines were not quite *au point* and their drivers were handicapped on Buenos Aires' twisting Palermo Park circuit. Lang was in a similar condition to the machines, somewhat out of touch in a new world where the top men raced more frequently than he had been required to in his heyday, while he was no longer quite so supremely fit physically as he had once been—he was balding and tending to be stout rather than massive. He must have been satisfied to snatch a brief lead in both races and to eventually finish second and third.

In the following year, however, the Stuttgart firm re-entered International racing with the Type 300SL; this sports car was to give Lang one more 'classic' victory. The team which went to Le Mans was their first official entry in the 24-hours since 1930; it was Lang's first night race and—as his brief (60-mile) excursion in the 1952 Mille Miglia can be discounted—his first long-distance race. But the event suited his South German temperament, with Riess he drove a controlled race, leaving the drama and failures to others, and won.

A subsequent 'demonstration race' run as a prelude to the German Grand Prix gave Lang the satisfaction of a second Nürburgring victory and in gaining it, perhaps inspired by old associations, he at last showed something of his pre-War thrust and brilliance. It was sheer perseverance though, which pulled him stage by stage up the leader board through the eight-day Carrera Panamericana until he was ultimately classified second overall.

For their 1954 return to Grand Prix racing, Mercedes-Benz must have wished for a German driver comparable to the Lang of 1939—as it was they owed their successes in that season as much to Juan Manuel Fangio as to the W.196. Lang was called to drive only once, in one last race on the 'Ring in the fourth car entered for the German Grand Prix. Practice seemed only to confirm that a great driver was going out with a whimper, for whereas Fangio fractionally improved on Lang's 1939 record, the record-holder could manage only 10 minutes 13·1 seconds which put him on the fifth row of the grid. Then for just a few laps in the race, he was the *spitzenfahrer* of old—for a quarter of the German Grand Prix he ran second, giving away just under a second a lap to Fangio. At half-distance he spun, just as he had in his first Nürburgring race nineteen years earlier. This time he could not restart . . .

So Hermann Lang returned to family life in Bad Cannstatt, working as a service inspector for Mercedes-Benz. Occasionally, when a W.163 is run as a public relations exercise, he again drives the car of his magnificent peak year.

The principal racing successes of **HERMANN LANG**

1937	1st:	Avusrennen; Tripoli G.P.
	2nd:	Italian G.P.; Swiss G.P.
	3rd:	Belgian G.P.
1938	1st:	Coppa Ciano; Tripoli G.P.
	2nd:	German G.P.; Pau G.P.; Donington G.P.
	3rd:	French G.P.
1939	1st:	Belgian G.P.; Swiss G.P.; Eifelrennen; Pau G.P.; Tripoli G.P.
1950	2nd:	Solitude G.P.
1951	2nd:	Peron Cup.
	3rd:	Eva Peron Cup.
1952	1st:	Le Mans 24-hour Race; Nürburgring sports car race.
	2nd:	Carrera Panamericana.

A ghost of a smile even when 'serious' . . .

BERND ROSEMEYER

by CYRIL POSTHUMUS

SOME drivers acquire their skill by assiduous application to the job. Others are 'naturals', endowed with a genius which lesser men lack. Fangio, Ascari, Moss and Clark are obvious 'naturals' of recent years; Nuvolari and Caracciola of an earlier era. All these drivers enjoyed lengthy careers in which to establish their ascendancy, but there was another who shot meteor-like across the motor racing firmament, driving three short but shattering seasons before his light went out—a fair-haired young German from Lingen, Lower Saxony, named Bernd Rosemeyer, whose feats with the big 750-kg. rear-engined Auto Union (he raced no other cars) made him as legendary and unforgettable a figure to his countrymen as Nuvolari is to the Italians.

Like that great *maestro*, and so many other top-line drivers, Rosemeyer began by racing motor cycles. And like so many Germans between the wars, he had a hard time making ends meet. But he was a happy, buoyant character with an impetuous kind of skill which gained him several wins in local races and hill-climbs, riding BMWs and NSUs, until the DKW factory team signed him on.

Thus he joined the two-wheeled 'Continental circus' wherein so many talented young riders acquire their skill and know-how. DKW of course belonged to the recently formed Auto Union group, and as a member of the bike team, young Bernd heard much about the revolutionary new Grand Prix cars being built in the Horch works at Zwickau. These had 16-cylinder engines installed at the rear, independent suspension, aeroplane-type bodies—the rumours excited him, and so did the reality when the cars made their eventual appearance in 1934, and their star driver, the Austrian Hans Stuck, won the German, Swiss and Czech Grands Prix and did splendidly elsewhere. Bernd practically burst for the chance to drive one, and pestered the Auto Union team manager Willy Walb until, in November, he was given a trial.

On the great day, he turned up at the Nürburgring wearing a lounge suit. 'Where are your overalls?' asked Walb. 'Well, this is a great occasion for me—my première in a racing car—so I thought I'd dress for it,' quipped Bernd.

'Get some overalls on, and get into the car,' said Walb shortly 'and drive slowly—the first laps are for getting used to things, not for records.' Off went Rosemeyer, feeling his way in the big, squat, silver Auto Union. But he knew his 'Ring well, and turned a surprisingly good first lap time. His second lap was faster and then Bernd, handling ten times more horsepower than he'd ever known, learned how unforgiving the rear-engined A.U. could be if one took liberties. Coming through one of Nürburg's incessant bends he put the power on too quickly, the back swung round, the car spun twice and ended up in a meadow, its engine still running. Bernd drove back to the pits, there to counter Walb's accusing eye by pointing at his car and saying, 'Imagine it—

. . . but more often a grin

129

she wanted to take me for a walk. Now I'm going to take *her* for one,' and off he went again to set a lap time unequalled by any Auto Union driver other than Stuck. They signed him on as reserve driver.

Walb couldn't be angry with this carefree youngster, who infected the whole team with his gay laughter. But he hardened his heart when the 1935 season began and Bernd began to clamour for a drive. The Tunis and Tripoli races passed and next came the Avus G.P. outside Berlin, when Walb again indicated that he would not need Rosemeyer's services. 'Too fast and too dangerous for a new driver,' he said, but Bernd had raced big BMW motor cycles there and thought otherwise.

Notes began to appear each day on Walb's desk calender: 'Wird Rosemeyer auf der Avus Fahren?' ('Will Rosemeyer drive on the Avus?'). Then 'Why is Rosemeyer not driving yet?', 'Where is the car for Rosemeyer?' and 'Rosemeyer *will* drive on the Avus.' At last Walb exploded and wrote 'Ja!' furiously beneath, and Bernd got his drive. His best practice lap at over 153 m.p.h. was third fastest of all amongst very *élite* company, but his race was spoiled, first by a thrown tread when he held his car most skilfully, and finally by a burst engine.

Obviously this 25-year-old recruit had talent; equally obviously he was not afraid of high speed. His next race made him famous overnight. It was the Eifelrennen on his beloved Nürburgring, and although Bernd was only Number Four in the team, fate played his way; Varzi was sick, Stuck's car *went* sick and Pietsch was too far back. With three Mercedes out in front, Dr. Porsche and Willy Walb had no choice but to signal their new boy to go 'faster'.

Carte blanche to go flat out—what joy for the irrepressible Bernd. A pebble smashed his screen, another his goggles, but he responded magnificently, slinging his Auto Union through the corners in great slides and passing Chiron and Fagioli to close on the great Caracciola himself. Nose to tail they raced for lap after lap, until race leader von Brauchitsch blew up and Bernd passed Caracciola to find himself in the lead! But 'Carratsch' was too experienced to be ousted so easily; he caught his young rival less than a mile from the finish to win for Mercedes by 1·8 seconds. Even so, German race fans had a new idol. . . .

There was no more nonsense about his being reserve driver after that—he became Number Three to Hans Stuck and Varzi, and his progress through the rest of the season was electrifying, sometimes lurid. Having 'mixed it' with Caracciola, he next tried it with another ace, Tazio Nuvolari. This was at Pescara in Italy, when he attempted to pass the master's Alfa Romeo on the second lap and skidded off-course instead, battering his tail and bursting both rear tyres against a bank. He limped to his pit, changed rear wheels and resumed. But Pescara, both fast and slow, is very hard on cars, and on lap 8 his brakes seized before a corner. The tail-heavy A.U. slewed viciously off the road, flattened a kilometre stone, leapt a ditch and passed between a telegraph pole and the parapet of a bridge before Bernd could get it back on the road. Yet he went on to finish second behind his team mate Varzi . . .

After the race, Dr. Porsche went to the scene of the spin, and measured the gap between the pole and the bridge. It was just 2½ cm. (one inch) wider than the Auto Union at its widest point! Silently Porsche shook hands with Bernd and patted his shoulder. Two 'thirds' at Berne and Monza followed, and then Rosemeyer had his first sweet taste of victory in the Masaryk G.P. in Czechoslovakia, winning by over six minutes from Nuvolari and Chiron.

The tail-heavy A.U. took over from his sensitive hands occasionally (Monaco, 1936) . . .

. . . but usually he had its measure (Eifelrennen, Nürburgring, 1937)

Nineteen-thirty-six was a Rosemeyer year almost from start to finish. 'Almost' only because the over-exuberant Bernd 'lost' his 520 b.h.p. Auto Union in the streaming wet at Monaco and finished up tail first hard against a stone balustrade, and because at Tunis and Tripoli his car caught fire. But no other driver handled the unwieldy rear-engined cars as he did, though he never seemed to take his racing too seriously. It was a game to be enjoyed even when exacting circuits and formidable rivals demanded iron concentration. His perpetual laugh and gaiety endeared him to all at a time of mounting grimness for Germany. Full of nervous energy, he could seldom keep still; he would take a flying leap into his car rather than merely climb in like the languid Varzi. He would put out waggish pit signals to Caracciola giving improbable lap times, climb walls or trees and perform monkey tricks; once at Nürburg practice in front of the pits he put his car on full lock and opened the throttle hard, proceeding across the track in a series of ground loops.

His win in the fog in the 1936 Eifelrennen was an epic, during which he caught von Brauchitsch, Caracciola and Nuvolari in fair fight but foul weather, to win an at-times invisible race over the mist-cloaked Nürburgring. After that he was the *Nebelmeister*—master of the mists. A month later he won the German G.P. on the same course, following it up with victories in the Pescara, Swiss and Italian G.P.s, and emerged a true Champion of Europe.

Nineteen-thirty-seven was tougher. Varzi and Stuck were now past their prime and he was on his own for Auto Union without their top-line support, whereas Mercedes had a new and very fast car and an all-star cast of drivers. Flying treads cost him the Tripoli G.P., and failing oil pressure the Avus race; but he won the Eifelrennen again, then crossed the Atlantic to win the Vanderbilt Cup on Long Island.

The Americans thought the gay young Saxon was *wunderbar*, but he thought their circuit was terrible. Against virtual 4 to 1 odds he then beat the Mercedes team at Pescara and in the Donington G.P., where his inspired driving thrilled 50,000 British fans.

That Donington event was his thirteenth and final race of 1937. None could know that glorious autumn day that it was destined to be the last race of his life. He died, not in the heat of battle during a Grand Prix, but in a pointless quest for a speed record already held by a German car. Driving an ultra-streamlined Auto Union on the Frankfurt–Darmstadt Autobahn on January 28, 1938, he essayed to beat new Class B figures just set up by Caracciola in a Mercedes at over 268 m.p.h. A strong side wind was blowing as he rocketed through the measured distance; at maximum velocity the Auto Union suddenly lurched into a terrible skid. A tyre flew off, the Auto Union somersaulted, flinging Rosemeyer out, then dashed itself to pieces against a concrete bridge. They found him unmarked but dead, his face calm and peaceful, his young life squandered through national inter-marque rivalry.

He was buried with full military honours. Hitler said to the German people 'May the thought that he fell fighting for Germany's reputation lessen your grief.' It didn't. Germans in their hundreds still attend the annual memorial service at the simple stone marking the spot where he met his death—his widow Elly Beinhorn, former famous airwoman, his son Bernd, relatives and friends, officials and colleagues from Auto Union, members of the DKW Club and other admirers of a very great driver.

Last race, Donington, 1937

Coppa Acerbo winner, 1936

The principal racing successes of **BERND ROSEMEYER**

1935	1st:	Masaryk G.P.		2nd:	Hungarian G.P.
	2nd:	Eifelrennen; Coppa Acerbo.	1937	1st:	Eifelrennen; Coppa Acerbo; G. Vander-
	3rd:	Italian G.P.; Swiss G.P.			bilt Cup; Donington G.P.
1936	1st:	German G.P.; Italian G.P.; Swiss G.P.;		2nd:	Grosvenor G.P.; Tripoli G.P.
		Coppa Acerbo; Eifelrennen.		3rd:	German G.P.; Italian G.P.; Masaryk G.P.

WILBUR SHAW

by AL BLOEMKER

'*Anything you can do, I can do better!*'

That was Wilbur Shaw's unvarying attitude towards each challenge offered him during his exciting career—an all-inclusive statement covering every type of accomplishment from displays of physical prowess, dexterity and tricks of magic to the more important tasks of building and driving fast race cars.

Now, after his tragic death in an aeroplane crash on October 30, 1954, his name remains high on the all-time list of America's greatest drivers and his many important contributions to the popularity of racing in the United States remain unequalled.

His record as a competitor includes three Indianapolis '500' victories and he was the first to capture the big prize in two consecutive years.

His unparalleled work as a 'goodwill ambassador' provided the impetus for the sport's amazing growth following the economic depression of the 1930s and the four-year suspension of competition due to the Second World War.

His perseverance and enthusiasm saved the Indianapolis Motor Speedway from a fate similar to that which engulfed Brooklands and other famous courses.

And the continued success of the Indianapolis 500-mile Race as the 'world's greatest sports spectacle' under the direction of Tony Hulman can be traced directly to Shaw's personal guidance during the last nine years of his life as the Speedway's president and general manager.

Unlike most of his contemporaries, Wilbur attained his objectives 'the hard way', with the aid of amazing self-reliance acquired by necessity at an early age when his parents were divorced. Despite his lack of formal education—he dropped out of high school before completing his freshman year, to accept employment installing batteries for the Stutz Company in Indianapolis—he grasped every opportunity to increase his knowledge about all aspects of automobile engineering while gaining valuable practical experience by the trial-and-error method.

Opportunity was a word of particular importance in Shaw's vocabulary, because he had the uncanny knack of recognizing it in almost any form in which it presented itself. But his success was due primarily to his natural ability, dauntless determination, competitive spirit, unquestioned courage and to a great deal of hard work combined with a personal charm which opened many doors often found locked by other members of the racing profession.

Access to tools, with which to start building his first race car on his own time at night, prompted him to quit his job at Stutz to become Bill Hunt's 'helper' at Imperial Motors (at a drastic cut in his weekly pay). Hunt was a regular campaigner on the Fronty-Ford circus which covered the half-mile dirt tracks of Indiana, Ohio and Illinois. This association enabled Shaw to become acquainted with other drivers and he salvaged the worn-out spare parts they discarded until in 1921 as an ambitious 18-year-old youngster he had acquired enough to build a car of his own, even though he realized it would be one of very questionable quality.

It failed to pass the technical inspection when he entered it in competition for the first time at the Hoosier Motor Speedway's half-mile dirt course on the outskirts of Indianapolis. But officials at a similar track near Lafayette, Indiana, weren't so particular two weeks later. Under the lax rules which existed at that time, they even permitted Hunt to qualify the car for Shaw, when Wilbur experienced difficulty familiarizing himself with the course during the brief practice period available.

Hunt's performance was good for a starting spot on the outside of the front row. Wilbur led the pack through the first turn of the oval track and down the backstretch. But he was travelling too fast to negotiate the second turn safely, his car hit a rut, crashed through the fence and landed upside-down. Shaw escaped injury only by 'scooting down in the basement' and clinging to the steering column.

His persistent search for 'another ride' culminated in a chance to drive a Fronty Ford of better quality for Roscoe E. Dunning later in the same season and Shaw's first race in the car was a winning one. His reward for leading the field home in a ten-lap event on the same Lafayette track where he had wrecked his own car was only $18, but that was sufficient for him to regard himself as a full-fledged professional driver.

Other victories followed quickly in the RED Special (a name formed by using Dunning's initials); by the end of the 1926 season, which for him reached its climax with a record-breaking triumph in a 100-mile dirt-track race on Chicago's Hawthorne oval, Wilbur was impatient to challenge the nation's outstanding veterans on the American Automobile Association's championship circuit.

Although he drove an outmoded three-year-old car to fourth place in his first Indianapolis '500' appearance the following May, he discovered it was almost impossible to get a 'regular ride' in new equipment comparable to that provided for most of his more experienced rivals. His record for the remainder of the summer was disappointing. The 1928 season also started on a 'sour note' when the owner of the Indianapolis car, which had been promised to Shaw, sold it to a rival who preferred Lou Meyer as driver. Wilbur finally was given a chance to qualify for the annual event in a hastily repaired car which had been wrecked by Pete De Paolo during practice, but it lasted only forty-two laps because of timing gear trouble.

A crushing emotional blow at this stage of Wilbur's career—the loss of his wife in premature childbirth—apparently drained him of all incentive to excel at anything. But within three months he was back on the half-mile dirt tracks, under suspension by the AAA Contest Board and with a 'don't give a damn' attitude that lasted until a new romance rekindled his desire to become a champion.

He obtained reinstatement as an AAA driver in good standing, effective on May 26, 1929, with the additional stipulation that he could not compete in the Indianapolis Classic on May 30, and didn't waste a single moment resuming his determined climb towards the pinnacle of racing. In rapid succession he won six of the first seven 100-mile AAA dirt track contests for which he was eligible and led all rivals in a 200-

miler on the Altoona board oval until fumes from a faulty supercharger forced him to ask for relief.

Victory at Indianapolis, his primary objective, didn't come quickly. But he remained undaunted despite many disappointments. After crashing over the wall in a Duesenberg early in the 1931 event, he walked back to the pit area and resumed the battle as a relief driver for Jimmy Gleason thirty minutes later.

He shrugged off such accidents with the philosophy of a fatalist. 'When my time finally comes,' he told friends, 'It isn't going to matter whether I'm driving a race car, flying a plane, or sitting at home in an easy chair.'

Following Duesenberg's withdrawal from racing, he drove Miller-powered cars, finishing second at Indianapolis in 1933 and again in 1935. For 1936, he built his own car and it was finished barely in time to qualify for a '500' starting position despite a painful hand injury which forced him to rely on others for part of the body works. At 200 miles he led the second-place car by 1 minute 21 seconds with all other rivals trailing by at least two full laps. But one of Shaw's volunteer helpers had omitted the important step of bolting the hinges securely to the radiator shell before riveting the hood panels into position. They ripped loose as Shaw started to lap Ralph Hepburn for the third time and a 17-minute pit stop was necessary for repairs.

The fact that Shaw's 'corrected time', computed by subtracting pit time from elapsed time, was 4 minutes and 15 seconds faster than that of the winner, provided little consolation for he collected $3,650 for seventh place instead of the top prize which amounted to more than $30,000.

Wilbur's faith in his own car was justified the following year when he scored the first of his three Indianapolis triumphs—nosing out Hepburn by 2·16 seconds in a dramatic finish at a record-breaking speed of 113·580 miles an hour.

While participating in the 300-mile event on the road course at New York's Roosevelt Raceway later in the season, however, against the best drivers and machines from Europe, Wilbur became entranced with the performance of the eight-cylinder, 3-litre supercharged Maseratis. He persuaded Mike Boyle of Chicago to order such a car for the 1938 Indianapolis classic. However, a misunderstanding resulted in delivery of a 1·5-litre model, which Wilbur rejected in favour of his own car. Believing that an average of 115 m.p.g. would be ample to win the '500' again, he made no attempt to match the early speed displayed by Floyd Roberts and had to be content with second place when Roberts continued without trouble for a new race record at a speed of 117·20 m.p.h.

Boyle's chief mechanic, 'Cotton' Henning, made a personal trip to Italy during the winter months and returned with a 3-litre 8 CTF Maserati which was everything Shaw had hoped it would be. He won at Indianapolis, despite an emergency stop for fuel with only nine laps to go, and repeated the triumph in 1940 to match Meyer's three '500' victories while at the same time earning the distinction of becoming the first driver to lead the field home for two consecutive years.

Another triumph with the Maserati appeared to be assured in 1941. Only forty-eight laps remained, he already had made his last scheduled pit stop and he enjoyed a lead of more than a lap on all rivals. Contracts worth more than $150,000, for his endorsement of certain products

K

as the only four-time Indianapolis winner, awaited his signature. But the spokes of the Maserati's right rear wheel pulled loose at the hub and sent him crashing, tail first, into the concrete retaining wall on the outer edge of the No. 1 turn.

Shaw recovered rapidly from his injuries and soon resumed his duties with Fireston's aircraft division—a position he had taken in the previous autumn with the promise of a leave of absence for his annual appearance in the Indianapolis race. But there was little time to think of racing until the end of the Second World War when with the cessation of hostilities in Europe, Firestone asked Wilbur to make a special 500-mile test of a new type of synthetic on the Speedway course.

What he saw on his arrival at the track was extremely disheartening. Big crevices in the surface required patching before the test could get under way; grass and weeds grew between the bricks on the main straight; old wooden grandstands looked as if they would fall apart in the first stiff breeze and it was apparent that no maintenance work of any kind had been done for four years.

Investigation revealed that Captain Eddie Rickenbacker, then the Speedway president, was not interested in tackling the expensive task of restoring the Brickyard to a condition suitable for a resumption of racing. Spurred by that knowledge, Shaw immediately launched a one-man crusade to preserve and renovate the scene of his greatest triumphs regardless of the cost in time and money. For many weeks he searched in vain for an individual or an organization willing to provide financial support, until finally he managed to interest the young, aggressive, civic-minded, industrialist who headed Hulman and Company at Terre Haute, Indiana.

As president and general manager of the Speedway, Wilbur watched with mingled emotions as the '500' was resumed in 1946. He couldn't

Traditional Speedway poses: in the Gilmore Special, 1937.

hide his disappointment at being on the sidelines as his rivals of long
standing started another spectacular charge towards the chequered
flag which awaited one of their number at the finish. But he gloried in
the fact that his 'beloved 500' had been saved from its impending
doom; and he worked tirelessly until his death to establish the
foundation on which the 'World's Greatest Sports Spectacle' now
stands so firmly.

in the 'Boyle Special' Maserati 8CTF, 1940

First World Champion (*1950*)

GIUSEPPE FARINA

by GIOVANNI LURANI

NINO FARINA to all motorists, Doctor Giuseppe Farina officially (as he got his full law degrees at the Turin university), among the living retired champions of the past, perhaps survived more racing accidents than any other famous driver. The long and awe-inspiring list of these accidents is due (in part at least) to his fighting temperament, his exceptional courage and a fiery determination that was sometimes even mistaken for ruthlessness. The fact that he has survived all of them to bear, as a reminder, a fair amount of scars (he does not even remember how many accidents he was involved in let alone which wound is a souvenir of which) is probably also due to a more than fair share of good luck.

Giuseppe, or Nino Farina, was born in Turin, October 30, 1908, and his father was the oldest of the Farina brothers who had founded the famous coachbuilding business in Turin. Later on the brothers split their business and the cars built in the works of Nino Farina's father were marked with a capital 'F', while those built in his uncle Pinin Farina's works, were marked with a small 'f' (later on the death of Nino Farina's father and contemporary business conditions led to the closure of the 'F' works and now only the small 'f' survives, famous throughout the world).

A very handsome young man in his early twenties, Nino Farina was a brilliant cavalry officer during his military service (and many times was mistaken for the Prince of Piedmont, then Crown Prince and later King Umberto of Italy!). He was already driving cars (his first was a twin-cylinder Temperino) when nine years old. He was also a good cyclist, a good soccer player and a track athlete but his real love was to be motor racing even if he was also for many years a first class skier as well, during the then 'dead season' of winter.

Eager to race . . . (*Monaco, 1937*)

While still a student, he made some pocket money with a lucky stock exchange gamble, and with a little help from his father, he bought a second-hand 1,500-c.c. Alfa Romeo. He promptly smashed it in his very first 'race', the Aosta-Grand St. Bernard hill-climb; in the same event his father finished fourth—Nino finished in hospital with a broken shoulder and some cuts in his very hard skull!

His enthusiasm was not impaired by this accident, and his determination increased. In the years 1933 and 1934 he drove private Maserati and Alfa Romeo cars with impressive results. Win or burst was his motto. In 1934, at a Turin hill-climb in which I also was competing, he overturned his eight-cylinder Alfa Romeo half a mile after the start!

But all the while his driving style was improving and his very evident keeness and stamina impressed the great Tazio Nuvolari who took a liking to the young man, started to protect him and became thus his worshipped teacher. Under the tuition of the *Maestro* Farina was to become one of the star drivers of that rich period in Italy when men of the calibre of Nuvolari himself, Varzi, Fagioli, Brivio, Trossi, Biondetti were all racing internationally. With Chiron, Etancelin, Caracciola, Stuck, Rosemeyer, Lang and company, they formed a galaxy of talent since unequalled on the circuits at any one time.

In the pre-war years, the German cars were unbeatable, but Farina was often on their heels, sometimes second, and many times first in minor races. He drove in the famous Mille Miglia many times, but his best result in this race was 'mere' second place in the wake of team-mate Brivio's Alfa Romeo when he had to drive in the night with no lights, following other cars and relying on theirs in the pitch dark. Winner of the Turin, Milan and Naples Grands Prix in 1937, in 1938 he was second to Lang in the Coppa Ciano, to Caracciola in the Coppa Acerbo at Pescara and to Nuvolari in the Italian Grand Prix, thus becoming official Italian Champion of the year.

In 1939, as Number One driver in the Alfa Romeo team, he was again Italian Champion and won several races but his best performance was undoubtedly his incredible race with the 1½-litre supercharged 'Alfetta' in the Swiss Grand Prix on the treacherous Bremgarten circuit. Against the formidable teams of 3-litre Mercedes and Auto Unions he took full advantage of conditions to offset a power deficit of more than two to one. In driving rain, on the skid-pan surface of the deadly circuit, Nino more than managed to stay with the German cars and gloriously and rather impudently held second position for many laps, forfeiting it only when the roads dried.

After the war, Farina was already a veteran (in company with Villoresi and Taruffi, while Fagioli and Nuvolari were in their last active period), but he was more than ever dedicated to racing—and to winning. In 1946 he drove an 'Alfetta' to victory in the Grand Prix des Nations at Geneva. In 1948 he drove Maseratis, winning the Monaco G.P., in the Argentine and in Switzerland.

In 1949 he drove Ferraris and Maseratis but in 1950 he returned to the colours of Alfa Romeo, then at the height of their fame with the Type 158/159. Trossi had gone, so had Wimille, and the famous 'Three

Grand Prix Alfas. German G.P., 1937 . . .

Fs' team started its short but glorious career. The 'Three Fs' were Farina, Fangio (then a 'comingman') and veteran Fagioli. The year 1950 was the first one in which the World Championship was competed for under the rules that are more or less those that are in force nowadays and which were inspired by the example set by the F.I.M. (motor cycling's international authority). Winning at Silverstone, at Monza and at Berne, well placed in the other Championship events, Farina was declared World Champion for 1950 and probably reached the climax of his career in that year.

He again drove Alfa Romeos, and Maseratis, in 1951. In 1952, when Alfa Romeo gave up Grand Prix racing, he joined Ascari and Villoresi in the Ferrari team and was up to his best against them and other stars — Fangio, Gonzalez, Moss and the veteran Taruffi.

One of his best races was surely the German Grand Prix of 1953 on the Nürburgring. His team-mate Ascari was in the lead with a good margin (more than 30 seconds) over Fangio (Maserati) while his other team-mate Mike Hawthorn was running third and Farina was fourth. Then came one of those incidents that make history. Ascari lost a front wheel and reached the pits on the brake drum, Fangio forged ahead in the lead in front of Hawthorn, trying hard to keep first place. Then Nino Farina got one of those fits of 'lion heart' and started to make up lost ground. Lapping on the limit he managed to pass not only his team-mate Hawthorn but also the great Argentinian ace, and thus win for Ferrari another Grand Prix.

In 1954 Farina led the Ferrari team and had great hopes, but this was to be one of his most unlucky seasons. At Syracuse, at the beginning of the year, he won the Grand Prix but only at great risk to his life when he managed to pass between the burning cars of Gonzalez and Hawthorn, only by driving through a real pin-hole with extreme precision and skill. But later in the season, while driving a 5-litre 350 h.p. 12-cylinder Ferrari in the Mille Miglia, he crashed at very high speed when in the lead. The car was written off and Farina was out of commission until June. On his next outing in practice at Monza with a 3-litre Ferrari for the 1000 km. race, a joint broke, the tank split and the car caught fire when travelling at full speed! Farina jumped as soon as the speed was low enough but was seriously burned. I collected him myself after the accident and drove him at speed to the hospital. He was obviously in great pain but his main worry was to find out when he could again drive a racing car!

This was to be in Argentina in 1955 when, still in pain, he had injections to be able to stand the gruelling race. And it was indeed a very tiring race in tropical heat; despite this Farina gallantly did his stint in the car which finished second.

Nino Farina was in many accidents, as I have already said; in some, outsiders were involved. In fact he crashed heavily in the Argentine (when the unruly spectators had practically invaded the track) and in Czechoslovakia; tragedies in which several people were killed. He was also mixed up in collisions with other cars during races and in two of these, the other drivers involved were fatally injured. Both occurred while Farina was overtaking and in both cases his car locked with another. The first also involved the Algerian driver Lehoux in the Deauville Grand Prix, the second the Hungarian champion Lazlo Hartmann in the 1938 Tripoli Grand Prix; Farina got away only superficially hurt while the other unfortunate drivers were killed. I too was

. . . Swiss Grand Prix, 1950

Determined, stylish (Belgian G.P., 1953)

driving in that Tripoli G.P. in 1938 and I remember passing between Farina's red Alfa Romeo, overturned and lying almost across the road, and poor Hartmann's Maserati also overturned and lying in the field on the other side of the road.

After a dramatic, colourful, dangerous and glorious career, Nino Farina has retired. He was active in the Italian distribution of Jaguar and then returned to Alfa Romeo in the same capacity. For some time he was chairman of the Competition Committee of the Turin Automobile Club and also tried to start a race driving school for young enthusiasts in Rome, but the scheme did not succeed.

But Nino Farina could be no 'school master' because he has always been a man driven by instinct. He never was a real 'scholar' of driving style as was for example, Piero Taruffi, or a spotless stylist and cold schemer like Varzi or Caracciola. He modelled himself on his 'idol' Nuvolari. From the *Maestro* he took the typical driving position with arms stretched out, and he always drove sitting back in the seat, with his head slightly inclined to one side, looking like an expert artist admiring a picture, the picture in this case being the road in front of his wheels. He made but light movements with his hands and arms, even in a period in which, by their characteristics, the cars he drove often required lots of correcting. Thus through experience and natural qualities, lightning-fast reactions and cold determination he acquired that style of driving that was admired everywhere but that he could never pass on to others.

He jumped starts quite a few times and in some races broke rear axles on the starting line. His nerves were unruly in those moments! But as soon as the race had really started there was Nino Farina, polished in his driving, fearless, completely devoted to his trade that was his whole life, capable of any performance, a complete driver (as Enzo Ferrari defined him), a man of steel—inside and outside—unscathed by the most appalling crashes, a champion in the real sense of the word.

The principal racing successes of **GIUSEPPE FARINA**

1933	3rd:	Naples G.P.
1934	1st:	Masaryk Voiturette Race.
	2nd:	Modena Voiturette Race.
	3rd:	Biella Circuit; Littorio Gold Cup.
1935	2nd:	Circuit of Bergamo.
	3rd:	Biella Circuit.
1936	3rd:	Milan G.P.; Modena f.l. Race; Penya Rhin G.P.
1937	1st:	Naples G.P.
	2nd:	Milan G.P.; Valentino G.P.
1938	2nd:	Italian G.P.; Coppa Acerbo; Coppa Ciano.
1939	1st:	Antwerp G.P.; Coppa Ciano; Prix de Berne.
	3rd:	Coppa Acerbo.
1940	1st:	Tripoli G.P.
	2nd:	Mille Miglia.
1946	1st:	G.P. des Nations, Geneva.
1948	1st:	Monaco G.P.; G.P. des Nations, Geneva; Circuit of Garda; Mar del Plata G.P.
1949	1st:	Lausanne G.P.; Rosario G.P.
	2nd:	Rio de Janeiro G.P.; International Trophy, Silverstone.

1950	1st:	British G.P.; Italian G.P.; Swiss G.P.; Bari G.P.; International Trophy, Silverstone.
	3rd:	Rosario G.P.
1951	1st:	Belgian G.P.; Paris G.P.; Ulster Trophy; Goodwood Trophy; Woodcote Cup, Goodwood.
	2nd:	Festival of Britain Trophy, Goodwood;
	3rd:	Italian G.P.; Spanish G.P.; Swiss G.P.; Pau G.P.
1952	1st:	Autodrome G.P., Monza; Naples G.P.
	2nd:	Belgian G.P.; Dutch G.P.; French G.P.; German G.P.; Comminges G.P.; Paris G.P.; Rheims G.P.; Syracuse G.P.
1953	1st:	German G.P.; Naples G.P.; Rouen G.P.; Nürburgring 1000 km; Buenos Aires G.P.; Silverstone f.l. Race.
	2nd:	Dutch G.P.; Italian G.P.; Swiss G.P.
	3rd:	Autodrome G.P., Monza; British G.P.
1954	1st:	Syracuse G.P.; Agadir Sports Car G.P.; Casablanca 12 Hours; Buenos Aires 1000 km.
	2nd:	Argentine G.P.
	3rd:	Buenos Aires G.P.
1955	2nd:	Argentine G.P.
	3rd:	Belgian G.P.

The Old Man

JUAN MANUEL FANGIO

by FEDERICO KIRBUS

IN Buenos Aires one fearful day in 1955 the thermometer stood at 104 degrees—in the shade, over 150 degrees on the track surface and probably nearly 180 degrees in the cockpits of the racing cars contesting the Argentine Grand Prix. By the time the race was over, only two of the original starters had been able to go the whole distance without relief. One of the two was thin, wiry Roberto Mieres (unfortunately fuel-pump trouble prevented him placing better than fifth). The other was Juan Manuel Fangio.

Fangio pulled Mercedes' chestnuts out of the fire that day. From start to finish, the scarlet Ferraris tried to get ahead, but Farina, Gonzalez and Trintignant fell back time after time, overcome by the heat—things got to the point where one of the cars was retired because there was no one left to drive it!

Nor were things any better *chez* Mercedes. Youngsters Stirling Moss and Hans Herrmann fell repeatedly by the wayside and left oldster Fangio, 44 at the time, to go straight through the race with a single pit stop. Juan still has scars on his leg to testify to the burns he received that day.

That Argentine Grand Prix stays in my memory for two reasons. First and foremost, it strikingly demonstrated Fangio's resolute will to win and sheer physical stamina under gruelling conditions. Secondly, it was the first *grande épreuve* of a season in which I was privileged to accompany Fangio and the Mercedes team racing all over Europe.

Soon afterwards I got another glimpse into Fangio's character. After the Monaco G.P. the Grand Prix circus had moved on to Spa for the Belgian event, for a race whch was to be a trouble-free procession for the Mercedes team and which was also marked by one of the best drives in the career of driver-journalist Paul Frère, who for the occasion had been given the wheel of a Squalo Ferrari. I stationed myself at the la Source hairpin and settled down to study the individual drivers and their technique. By this time I was friendly with most of them and nearly all waved, gestured or made some sign that they had seen me—particularly Stirling Moss. Then Fangio came past and when he had gone I awoke to the realization of one of the things that makes Fangio what he is. Although he saw me clearly, although he had perforce to come slowly round the hairpin and although I was a friend of his and a fellow-countryman in a foreign land, he made not the slightest sign that he had recognized me. For when the flag fell to signal the start of a race, Juan forgot everything else; the world outside the tiny cockpit of his car just ceased to exist.

To make certain, I remained at la Source for some time, and not even a flicker disturbed the impassivity of Fangio's countenance as he went round time after time, cornering on exactly the same line, braking at exactly the same point, changing up after exactly the same number of seconds.

Roaring days. In the Ford Special, 1938

During a race Fangio's mind worked like a computer, assessing the car, the circuit, signals from his and his rivals' pits, his own physical reserves, what the other drivers were doing and how long there was to go. The information was fed in, processed, and telegraphed out to the hands and feet that worked like lightning on the sensitive controls of the Mercedes-Benz.

In race after race I was able to verify the theory that had been formed during that moment at la Source. During a race, nothing existed to Fangio but an absolute and whole-hearted dedication to his metier. Never once have I seen him smile, wink or even glance at anyone beside the circuit, much less lift a hand off the wheel to wave.

Was Fangio the greatest driver ever? Comparison is difficult. What is surprising is that Fangio became so great in the tricky and agile single-seaters, which require immense delicacy of touch. Surprising because he learned to drive in the thundering 'Turismo Carretera' modified and Chevrolet coupés which still hurtle along the unmetalled roads of Argentina. Weighing a good ton and a half, usually fitted with beam axles front and rear, and seldom the latest things as far as road-holding is concerned—this was particularly so in the late thirties when Fangio was active in this type of road racing—the Turismo Carretera coupés are hardly calculated to teach finesse.

And yet, Juan won the World Championship five times in Grand Prix Monoposti, where inches count, where an unnecessary flick of the wheel may mean a spectacular slide off the track. Even stranger is the fact that, as far as sports cars were concerned, Stirling Moss was without a doubt a better driver than Juan Manuel. Not that the difference was very great, of course, because I am personally convinced that Fangio could have been a star driver on anything on wheels. But I have always thought that in those unforgettable days when they raced together or against each other, Moss was a shade better where two-seaters were concerned. Which was definitely not the case as regards single-seaters.

Every one of us may be born with a fixed destiny already written out—but whatever way considered, it is a far cry from a bucking, bouncing Chevrolet coupé flying along an unmetalled road to a 250F Maserati!

Half a dozen years after that eye-opening Belgian Grand Prix I saw Fangio slide into the cockpit of a rear-engined car of another generation and, unused to the ultra-responsive steering, weave from side to side of the road as if he was learning to drive. Of course, it didn't take him very long to get things straight and drive as if he'd been born and bred to racing Formula Junior racing cars.

Would Fangio have been a star today? The matter lends itself to considerable argument. Without a doubt, a good driver in one type of vehicle can drive a different type well or at least learn to do so with ease and alacrity. However, when Fangio started out on his spectacular European career, he was 'almost forty and almost fat'. To be precise he was 38 and, in spite of constant exercise and Spartan living, rapidly developing a middle-age spread. The way things are today, this fact alone would have meant a considerable handicap to him, as it would have to González, Ascari and even Farina, none of whom were exactly slim Apollos. Look at the men who win the World Championships today . . .

In all probability, Fangio's career would have been far less meteoric had he started racing ten years later. However, it is hardly fair to use that argument against him when one considers whether or not he was the finest driver the world has ever known. There are too many variables to take into account. In any case one fundamental fact would be remembered; Fangio is a smart man, an intelligent man. He was clever enough to foresee which would be the fastest cars at the start of each season, and skilful enough to make up for any slight error in his first judgement. He was also intelligent enough to retire when at the peak of his career, before the years began to take their toll of his reflexes. Others unhappily, were not, and paid for it with spectacular crashes or a decline into mediocrity.

However, when one compares the drivers of the sixties with those of the fifties, one must not forget that the 250F Maseratis and four-cylinder Ferraris were incomparably harder to drive than the sure-footed little vehicles of today. They were certainly powerful, yet their road-holding, by today's standards, was indifferent, and their braking also fell far short of what is nowadays acceptable. Carlos Menditeguy has told me of stepping from a 250F Maserati into a Cooper-Climax, using the 'Maserati' cut-off and braking points, and finding himself practically at a dead stop in the middle of the straight!

Taking everything into account, I think that Fangio was the almost-perfect driver of his day. Were he to be in G.P. racing today, I do not think he would be any better than extremely good. Juan dropped out of racing just about the time the little rear-engined cars were beginning to show their teeth. Perhaps he was wise enough to see the writing on the wall. Appropriately enough, Fangio's last great race marked the first big-time win for a Cooper; the Argentine Grand Prix won by Stirling Moss. To use a trite phrase, 'I can almost see him now', Fangio's Maserati powersliding, slithering, wasting energy on the bends while the little dark blue Cooper (a Rob Walker entry, historians will recall) minnowed its way in and out of the bends almost like a model.

These older cars were harder to drive, but they allowed a tiny fraction of a second in which to correct mistakes made when choosing the line in to a bend. The little cars of the present corner so well that this facility no longer exists; more people can drive well, but when the Grand Masters start wringing out the last fractions of a second, the penalty for mistakes is swift and sure, almost as in motor cycle racing in which it is impossible to change your line once you have committed yourself.

Fangio must be viewed in the context of his day and of the tremendous influence he had in the style of driving of that time. I think that Fangio was the man who really showed the way to wide, sweeping four-wheel drifts in heavy and relatively intractable cars like the Alfetta, the early 4CLT/48 Maseratis, and later the W.196 Mercedes-Benz and the V-8 Ferrari (a particular beast, this one). Although only a few years have gone by, we can already look back on that era as heroic. Without doubt, races were far more fun to watch, although the cars of today have reached a seemingly incredible peak of technical perfection.

In spite of his hairy-sounding lap records, Fangio was a very safe driver. In fact he had only two accidents; once, in 1952, in Monza, when he started when almost on the brink of physical exhaustion (a valuable lesson, this), and later, in 1953, when he had re-entered racing after his 1952 accident.

Impassive. Maserati, San Remo, 1949 . .

. . . Alfa Romeo, Swiss Grand Prix, 1950 .

. . . Maserati, Belgian Grand Prix, 1953 . . .

. . . Mercedes-Benz, French Grand Prix, 1954 . . .

. . . Lancia-Ferrari, German Grand Prix, 1956 . . .

. . . Maserati, French Grand Prix, 1957

It is not unlikely that the two incidents were connected, but they were the only two he ever had. Ironically enough, one of the worst moments of his career came when he was just going round 'for fun'. In one of the Argentine *Temporada* races in Córdoba, Central Argentina, a young Venezuelan driver told Juan that he was the present owner of a Maserati in which the World Champion had won several important races. Would Fangio like to drive the car again? He agreed and set off, but the engine cut out while Fangio was cornering hard and the car smote the kerb and reared up in the air. He carried on, but at the next curve discovered to his dismay that the previous *contretemps* had wiped out a hydraulic brake line, which, of course, is an unpleasant thing to happen while driving a racing car. Only the skill of a Fangio could have avoided an accident that time. And it did, luckily for Juan!

Above all things Fangio is fundamentally a natural driver, one who does the right thing intuitively. For instance, without the need for anybody to tell him so he discovered the correct posture for long-distance driving, elbows and knees at approximately 120 degrees angle. A fact which doctors only found out years afterwards . . .

Juan Manuel Fangio's origins were humble indeed. His father was a house painter of slender means, and at a tender age young Juan was apprenticed to a mechanic in order to learn a trade. Inevitably, he succumbed to the appeal of motor racing, and from wild and hairy rides in super-tuned Model T Fords he gradually progressed to *Turismo Carretera* Chevrolets, thence to home-built single-seaters with American power units and eventually to Grand Prix cars.

He visited Europe in 1948 but only started in one race in which he retired, without having particularly impressed anybody. In January 1949, however, he won his first victory against European Grand Prix drivers, with a 1,500-c.c. Maserati 4CLT/48. With this car, plus a 2-litre Ferrari which came later on, Fangio won his first four races in Europe and in all was placed first six times out of ten starts. By the end of 1949 he was already a figure to be reckoned with in Grand Prix racing.

So much so that for 1950 Alfa Romeos signed him up to drive the then invincible Alfettes, a remarkable guerdon for a driver so new to Europe. He barely missed winning the World Championship that year, but made sure of it in 1951.

In 1952 Fangio was driving for Maseratis; that year the Trident cars just weren't good enough to beat the Ferraris, and to cap it all Fangio had a serious accident in the Monza G.P. which kept him away from racing for several months. In 1953 he reappeared with Maseratis and, in spite of a wild off-course excursion in the Belgian G.P., snapped so successfully at Ferrari's heels that he managed to bag the last *grande épreuve* of 1953, and the last of the 2-litre Formula—the Italian Grand Prix, a wild event in which four drivers went round nose-to-tail until the very last lap, when everybody decided to spin at once and Fangio shot through the mêlée to bag first place!

Those years of the 2-litre Formula, '52 and '53, were Fangio's 'off years' but in 1954 he was back on top winning the Championship first with Maserati, then with Mercedes-Benz. In 1955 the Championship was in any case an all-Mercedes affair and as their Number One driver he naturally shared their rewards. In 1956, he won yet again, this time at the wheel of a Lancia-Ferrari; in 1957 he was World Champion for the fifth and last time, once again with Maserati.

Only occasionally did he show his reactions (V-16 B.R.M., Goodwood, 1953)

Last race (French Grand Prix, 1958)

He had a couple of starts in 1958, without attaining any special success, and wisely decided that the time had come to call it quits. It is singular, and one feels, very meritorious, that he never again started in so much as a saloon car race, although he does occasionally throw a sports car about when he gets the chance.

Today, Fangio is a big businessman, although he has never lost his quiet, retiring country ways. He handles millions today with the same coolness that stood him in good stead on racing circuits all over the world. His most recent project is a giant motel between Buenos Aires and Mar del Plata, Argentina's most important seaside resort, 250 miles away from the capital city.

He may no longer drive racing cars but, from his desk in Buenos Aires, Juan Manuel Fangio is still going places, fast.

The principal racing successes of **JUAN MANUEL FANGIO**

1939	1st:	Argentine 1000 km.
1940	1st:	G.P. of the North.
1941	1st:	Getulio Vargas G.P.; Argentine 1000 km.
1942	1st:	Rosario G.P.; Mar y Siera G.P.; Mar del Plata G.P.
1947	1st:	Spring G.P.; Prix Doble Vita.
1948	1st:	Vuelta de Pringles G.P.; Ontono G.P.
1949	1st:	Albi G.P.; Mar del Plata G.P.; Marseilles G.P.; Monza Autodrome G.P.; G.P. du Roussillon, Perpignan; Pau G.P.; San Remo G.P.
	2nd:	Buenos Aires G.P.; Argentine 1000 Miles; Eva Peron G.P.
1950	1st:	Belgian G.P.; French G.P.; Monaco G.P.; Argentine 500 Miles; Circuit des Remparts, Angoulême; G.P. des Nations, Geneva; Parana G.P.; Pau G.P.; Pescara G.P.; San Remo G.P.
	2nd:	Bari G.P.; International Trophy, Silverstone.
	3rd:	Mille Miglia.
1951	1st:	French G.P.; Spanish G.P.; Swiss G.P.; Bari G.P.
	2nd:	British G.P.; German G.P.
	3rd:	Buenos Aires G.P.; International Trophy, Silverstone.
1952	1st:	Argentine G.P.; Buenos Aires G.P.

1953	1st:	Italian G.P.; Carrera Panamericana; Modena G.P.
	2nd:	British G.P.; French G.P.; German G.P.; Mille Miglia; Pau G.P.; Naples G.P.; Woodcote Cup.
	3rd:	Bordeaux G.P.; Targa Florio.
1954	1st:	Argentine G.P.; Belgian G.P.; French G.P.; German G.P.; Italian G.P.; Swiss G.P.
	2nd:	Avusrennen.
	3rd:	Spanish G.P.
1955	1st:	Argentine G.P.; Belgian G.P.; Dutch G.P.; Italian G.P.; Buenos Aires G.P.; Eifelrennen; Venezuelan G.P.
	2nd:	British G.P.; Mille Miglia; Targa Florio; Tourist Trophy.
1956	1st:	Argentine G.P.; British G.P.; German G.P.; Mendoza G.P.; Sebring 12 Hours; Syracuse G.P.
	2nd:	Italian G.P.; Monaco G.P.; Nürburgring 1000 km; Venezuelan G.P.
	3rd:	Supercortemaggiore G.P.
1957	1st:	Argentine G.P.; French G.P.; German G.P.; Monaco G.P.; Portuguese G.P.; Buenos Aires G.P.; Cuban G.P.; Interlagos G.P.; Rio de Janeiro G.P.; Sebring 12 Hours.
	2nd:	Italian G.P.; Pescara G.P.
1958	1st:	Buenos Aires G.P.

L

World Champion, Morocco 1958

MIKE HAWTHORN

by PHILIP A. TURNER

WITHOUT doubt, Mike Hawthorn was one of the greatest amateur racing drivers of all time. The fact that he was paid by Ferrari, Vanwall, B.R.M. and other teams to drive their cars may have technically damaged his amateur status, but whether paid or not, he remained at heart an amateur. Mike raced not to make money, not to achieve a boyhood ambition to become world champion but because he loved racing. He delighted in battling wheel to wheel with some rival, time and again achieving the near impossible to stay ahead. He greatly enjoyed the company of his fellow drivers and felt thoroughly at home and at ease in the little tight world of motor racing. And he enjoyed the pressing attentions of the pretty girls who trail after well-known drivers, the same girls who in Spain toss flowers to their favourite matador in the arena. And who is to say their choice is any the poorer than the adoration of their sisters for film stars and pop idols?

Born at Mexborough in Yorkshire's West Riding on April 10, 1929, he in fact grew up in Surrey, for in 1931 his father, Leslie Hawthorn, bought the T.T. Garage at Farnham. Leslie moved his family south in order to be nearer to Brooklands where he raced motorcycles and then, like other motor cyclists such as Fred W. Dixon, took to four wheels by racing a Riley. Mike therefore grew up in a family in which fast cars were worshipped rather than looked on as sinful, and when in 1950 his father bought a 1,100-c.c. Riley Imp and a 1½-litre Riley Sprite, it was to enable Hawthorn *père et fils* to go motor racing. The family team made its first appearance at the Brighton Speed Trials, where Mike won the 1,100-c.c. class and father finished second in the 1½-litre category. A strained back the following year kept Leslie Hawthorn out of the 1½-litre Riley's cockpit, so Mike drove both cars at various meetings not only in England but also in the Ulster Trophy handicap race over the narrow, twisting Ballyclare circuit outside Belfast and the Leinster Trophy south of the border. Both of these he won with the Sprite, while his consistent success at B.A.R.C. Goodwood meetings gained him the *Motor Sport* Brooklands Memorial Trophy.

To the motor racing world at large, though, Mike was still just a promising club driver who had been going exceptionally well with a pair of pre-war Rileys in spite of their lack of independent suspension. It was his performance at the 1952 Goodwood Easter Monday meeting which made him a 'name' in one day. An old friend of the Hawthorn family, Bob Chase, bought one of the new front-engined 2-litre Cooper-Bristols for Mike to drive in Formula 2 races—in 1952 this was the supreme formula, for with the retirement of Alfa Romeo from Grand Prix racing, Formula 1 had lain down and died—and on that sunny April day before a record crowd of 50,000 Hawthorn shot straight out into the lead in the first race he had ever driven in a proper single-seater racing car with independent suspension and just stayed there for the whole six laps. Then he did it again in the six-lap Free Formula race.

Ulster, 1951

155

After this second race, I remember him sitting in his car in its paddock stall looking slightly abashed as the crowd thronged around his car and stared at the newcomer. Finally in the main race of the meeting, the twelve-lap Richmond Trophy, Hawthorn held a surprising second place in hot pursuit of Froilan Gonzalez in the 4½-litre Ferrari Thinwall Special and ahead of all the other Formula 1 cars. . . .

But rarely in the history of motor racing has a single meeting so changed the status of a driver, for Hawthorn was now a public figure. That his success at Goodwood was no mere flash in the pan was shown when he won the first heat of the *Daily Express* Silverstone meeting the following month, even though he retired with a broken gear lever when leading the final. Then in June, Hawthorn competed in his first Continental event, the Belgian G.P. on that beautiful but sinister Spa-Francorchamps circuit; he finished fourth, highest placed British driver and car. Hawthorn's third place in the British G.P. at Silverstone that year did not arouse so much comment as his third place in the Boreham International meeting. Here, in a combined 200-mile race for Formula 1 and Formula 2 cars which began in pelting rain, Hawthorn passed all the 4½-litre Ferraris and Lago-Talbots and the two V-16 B.R.M.s to lead the race for many laps. Only when the rain stopped and the circuit dried did Villoresi and Landi with the two Ferraris manage to re-pass the little Cooper-Bristol, which by now was also suffering from a loose flywheel.

This was indeed an eventful first season in the Big Time for Mike, for in addition to his races with the Cooper-Bristol, he competed in the works Sunbeam team in the Alpine Rally and won a coveted Coupe des Alpes in this, his first international rally. He tried a V-16 B.R.M., thought it horrid and drove Tony Vandervell's big 4½-litre Ferrari Thinwall Special instead in a race on the Scottish circuit of Turnberry (where ironically the B.R.M. won after the Thinwall had broken its rear axle).

This was the first association Mike had with B.R.M. at Bourne and with Tony Vandervell's Thinwalls. As yet, however, there were no B.R.M.s or Vanwalls for Hawthorn to drive in Grand Prix racing, nor were there any other British cars capable of challenging Ferrari or Maserati. In spite of the valiant efforts of H.W.M., Connaught and Cooper, the British cars were rarely higher than the third row of the starting grid for any of the championship Grands Prix. This situation faced Hawthorn with a very difficult problem, for it meant that if he was to make any further progress as a racing driver he would have to drive for a Continental team. Ferrari by the end of the season had offered him a place in what was without any doubt the foremost team in the world, but even so Hawthorn asked for time to think it over, hoping against hope that a British car capable of winning races would appear on the scene during the winter. Only when it was obvious this was not going to happen did Hawthorn sign a contract to drive the Italian cars.

In fact, he had plenty of time to contemplate the situation, as he spent the end of the season immured in hospital as a result of a crash at Modena while testing his Cooper-Bristol round this twisty little circuit. Only after a spell in the London Clinic, for fluid to be drained from one lung, did he recover.

During his first season for Ferrari Hawthorn drove in the Argentine races, the Mille Miglia and the Le Mans 24-hour Race as well as in the usual European Grands Prix, but without any shadow of doubt his

Making his mark, Boreham, 1952

Coming of age, French Grand Prix, 1953

outstanding race of the 1953 season was his tremendous victory in the French Grand Prix at Rheims. Hawthorn's wheel to wheel duel with Fangio's Maserati, how he snatched victory on the last corner of the last lap, this will be remembered as long as motor racing lives. Two weeks later he staged one of the most spectacular spins ever seen at Silverstone—and that's saying something—when in the British Grand Prix he lost the Ferrari coming out of Woodcote and took tail first to the grass in front of the grandstand at tremendous speed.

In spite of spinning almost the entire length of the pits, he was sufficiently professional to keep his engine running and thus was able to rejoin the race when the car had finished its gyrations.

It is probably true to say that Hawthorn's career reached a certain climax in 1954. He was the Golden Boy, who in one brief season had attained stardom. And then had justified that stardom by becoming the first Englishman since Sir Henry Segrave in 1923 to win the French Grand Prix.

By contrast, 1954 was a black year for Hawthorn. Right at the beginning of the season he crashed in flames in Syracuse and was badly burnt about the legs. Even when he returned to racing, some months later in the Belgian Grand Prix, his legs were still bandaged, and remained so for most of the season. Then the petty-minded little men who ever since the war had seemed to be dominant in victorious Britain, pursued Hawthorn in a mean campaign because he did not do his National Service, which was totally unjustified because the Services had already declared him unfit owing to a kidney complaint from which he had suffered since childhood. Plus two burnt legs. And finally, the father who had done so much to start Mike on his motor racing career rolled his Lancia one dark night when returning from a Goodwood meeting and never regained consciousness.

It is often forgotten how young, how very young, even the top racing drivers are. Hawthorn at this time was only 25, yet he was saddled with enough grief and disaster to flatten many an older man. Little wonder then, that in place of the laughing, carefree young man we had known hitherto, a somewhat bitter Hawthorn emerged with a rough and rather cynical outlook on the world outside motor racing.

Nor did 1955 do much to improve his outlook. Quite the reverse. In order to spend more time in England looking after the family garage business, Hawthorn left the Ferrari team to drive a Vanwall for Tony Vandervell. The Vanwall, however, was still in the development stage and was both unreliable and difficult to drive. After several disappointing performances, culminating in the Belgian Grand Prix, Hawthorn gave up the unequal struggle and reverted to Ferrari. Not that he was much better off, for the Ferraris were completely outclassed by the Mercedes W.196 team, but at least he managed to gain the occasional place.

But of course the most terrible incident of Hawthorn's entire career occurred in 1955, for it was in this year when, driving a works Jaguar, that he was involved in the great Le Mans disaster. The first two hours were the most dramatic motor racing I have ever witnessed, as for lap after lap Hawthorn's Jaguar fought with Fangio's Mercedes. Both drivers were on the limit, driving at the top of their very great skills with nothing whatsoever in reserve. Time and again Hawthorn lost the Jaguar but managed to regain control of the sliding dark green car and continue the pursuit of the massive silver Mercedes.

Then, after two hours, came Hawthorn's pit stop which by a tragic chain reaction resulted in the greatest disaster in motor racing history. An impartial committee of inquiry, after examining many witnesses and watching all available film of the accident, completely exonerated Hawthorn from blame. But their exoneration came many months after the accident, and in the somewhat hysterical aftermath determined attempts were made in some quarters to pin all the blame on Hawthorn. This campaign of vilification failed, thanks to the efforts of Hawthorn's friends, but once again poor Mike found himself the centre of a far from friendly stage.

That the campaign did not affect his fighting spirit was shown in September of that year when with the able partnership of Desmond Titterington, he took on the entire Mercedes team in the Tourist Trophy. The two drivers put up so great a fight that they totally disorganized the Mercedes machine and the German pit stops became chaotic. It was indeed sad that the hard-driven Jaguar engine broke its crank when the car was up in second place in the last laps of the race.

In order that he could continue to drive the works Jaguars in sports car races, Hawthorn left Ferrari at the end of the season and joined the B.R.M. team for 1956, thereby once again fulfilling his ambition to drive British. Alas, the new front-engined $2\frac{1}{2}$-litre B.R.M.s were in the same early stages of development as the Vanwall had been, but the cars were much more dangerous as they were already very fast, possibly the fastest G.P. cars of that season.

Having had quite enough near misses with the nascent B.R.M.s, Hawthorn returned with relief to Ferrari for the 1957 season and never again parted company with the team. It is, on the face of it, surprising that so English a character as Mike should seem to be really happy only in the Italian team, in spite of some pretty sharp arguments at times with successive Ferrari team managers. But then he found the sheer professionalism of the Italian team a very welcome contrast to the somewhat amateur approach to Grand Prix racing which at this time was a lamentable feature of the English teams.

Le Mans, 1955

*Before the last season turned sour.
British Grand Prix, 1958*

Back once more in the old familiar Italian surroundings it was as though Hawthorn had come home, and steadily throughout the 1957 and 1958 seasons the hurts he had suffered in the dark years seemed to heal and the bitterness left him. His final year of racing, 1958, brought him the great triumph of the World Drivers' Championship and the deep sadness of the death of his team mate and intimate friend, Peter Collins, in the German Grand Prix. Somehow, the sadness at last seemed to outweigh the glory and to the astonishment of most people he announced his retirement at the end of that season.

Hawthorn had no intention of severing all his connections with motor racing. He planned to put back into the sport a little of what he had gained from it by acting as marshal and generally lending a hand on the organization side, and it would not have been surprising if occasionally he had taken the wheel again at Vintage meetings. For Hawthorn, quite unlike so many current drivers of renown, was a tremendous motoring enthusiast. He spent many happy hours of his spare time rebuilding a 1931 2.3-litre Alfa Romeo and had carefully restored the 1½-litre Riley with which he began racing. And just before the 1957 Le Mans race he enjoyed himself immensely driving a borrowed 3-litre Bentley in a race for old cars staged on the Sarthe circuit. If only he had lived. . . .

But in January, 1959, his 3.8 litre Jaguar saloon went into an uncontrollable slide when travelling very fast downhill into Guildford and hit a tree. John Michael Hawthorn was killed instantly.

The principal racing successes of **J. M. HAWTHORN**

1951   1st: Leinster Trophy; Ulster Handicap.

1952   1st: *Daily Mail* Trophy (F.2) Boreham; Turnberry F.2 Race; Chichester Cup; Lavant Cup; Surrey Trophy, Goodwood; Ibsley f.l. Race.

      2nd: Ulster Trophy; Richmond Trophy, Goodwood.

      3rd: British G.P.; Empire Trophy.

1953   1st: French G.P.; Spa 24-hour Race; Pescara G.P.; Ulster Trophy; Goodwood Trophy; Woodcote Cup; International Trophy, Silverstone.

      2nd: Pau G.P.; Rouen G.P.

      3rd: German G.P.; Swiss G.P.; Buenos Aires G.P.

1954   1st: Spanish G.P.; Supercortemaggiore G.P.

      2nd: British G.P.; German G.P.; Italian G.P.; Portuguese G.P.; Tourist Trophy; *Daily Telegraph* Trophy, Aintree.

1955   1st: Le Mans 24-hour Race; Sebring 12 hours; Crystal Palace International Trophy.

      2nd: Supercortemaggiore G.P.; Oulton Park Gold Cup; *Daily Herald* International Trophy, Oulton Park.

1956   1st: Supercortemaggiore G.P.

      2nd: Rheims 12-hour Race; Whitsun Trophy, Goodwood.

      3rd: Swedish G.P.; Argentine G.P.

1957   2nd: German G.P.; Naples G.P.; Venezuelan G.P.

      3rd: British G.P.; Nürburgring 1000 km; Sebring 12 hours.

1958   1st: French G.P.; Glover Trophy, Goodwood.

      2nd: Belgian G.P.; British G.P.; Italian G.P.; Portuguese G.P.; Moroccan G.P.; Nürburgring 1000 km.

      3rd: Argentine G.P.; Targa Florio; Race of the Two Worlds, Monza.

PETER COLLINS

by GREGOR GRANT

WITH the tragic passing of Peter Collins, in the fateful 1958 German Grand Prix at Nürburgring, that band of gay cavaliers of the 1950's lost yet another of its number. He was just 27 years old, and within a few months his close friend Mike Hawthorn was fatally injured in a road accident.

To all of us who knew Pete, his accident on August 3, 1958, was inexplicable. He just didn't make errors, and it will always remain a mystery why he should have left the road with his Ferrari, whilst executing a manœuvre he had accomplished scores of times on that circuit, overtaking another car on a not particularly perilous bend. Hawthorn was dreadfully upset, so much so, that before the year was out, the new World Champion announced his retirement from motor racing. He no longer got the same kicks from racing, and missed the companionship of Collins far more than he was willing to admit.

Peter Collins was born into the world of motor cars, for his father, Patrick Collins, was a leading figure in the motor trade in Kidderminster. Fortunately for Pete, both Pat and Elaine Collins took the broad view that, if their son wanted to go motor racing, why he would go motor racing. As a result, when only 17 years of age, he proudly started his racing career with a Cooper-Norton '500' in 1949. By the following year, he had won the first Goodwood International Trophy race, and also the initial Silverstone 100-miles event. Speed hill-climbing also appealed to the young driver, and he secured many successes with twin-cylinder Cooper-J.A.P. machines. Even in those days, Collins displayed remarkable car control, and the sort of cool approach which stamped him as a man to watch.

In the beginning, Peter was something of a lone wolf, but gradually he lost his shyness, and quickly began to make friends. Amongst his closest acquaintances were Wing Commander Frank Aiken, Ron (Curly) Dryden and Alf Bottoms. The quartet joined forces to race Bottoms's venture, the JBS-Norton '500'. Alas, this project came to an untimely end, following fatal accidents to Bottoms at Luxembourg, and Dryden at Castle Combe.

Whether or not these tragedies influenced Peter Collins in his decision to abandon Formula 3 racing is debatable, but the fact remains that his interest in the class had gone, and when approached by the late John Heath, willingly agreed to join up with Stirling Moss and Lance Macklin in the H.W.M. Formula 2 team. His sojourn with H.W.M. provided him with the opportunity to gain experience in Grand Prix racing, and also brought his name to the notice of others.

The shrewd talent-spotter, the late Reg Parnell, saw immense possibilities in Peter Collins. Aston Martin team manager John Wyer agreed, and in 1952, Pete signed on to drive the David Brown sports-racing cars. With Pat Griffith he won the first Goodwood 'Nine Hours', and in the following year the same partnership gained victory in the

'Mon ami mate' – *with Mike Hawthorn, Supercortemaggiore G.P., 1956*

classic R.A.C. Tourist Trophy on the Dundrod circuit in Northern Ireland.

Another who admired Collins driving was Tony Vandervell, who entrusted him with the 4·5-litre Thin Wall Special Ferrari, which Vandervell had unashamedly acquired to play hell with B.R.M. plans for their V-16. This was a purely private dispute, arising out of certain differences of opinions connected with the administration of the original B.R.M. affairs, with which Tony Vandervell was connected. Anyway, Collins was an excellent choice for the *formule libre* races of the period, vanquishing the supercharged V-16 machines on several occasions. I well remember Pete running away with the *formule libre* race at Goodwood on Whit Monday, 1954; winning from B.R.M. again at Snetterton, and breaking the circuit lap record; leading all the way at Aintree, till mechanical trouble put him out. Collins and the Thin Wall almost broke the hearts of the men of Bourne.

Vandervell also entered Peter at Monza for the Italian G.P., in the original Vanwall, then fitted with a 2·2-litre engine. In this very experimental machine, first driven by Alan Brown at Silverstone as a 2-litre car, Collins managed to finish 7th.

Raymond Mays could not forget the trouble Collins had caused his B.R.M. drivers, and managed to secure his services to drive the new four-cylinder car at Oulton Park at the Gold Cup meeting. It was a sensational debut: for about 10 laps, the dark green B.R.M. led a formidable field containing such drivers as Hawthorn and Castellotti (Lancia-Ferraris), and Moss (Maserati) until a suspected fall in oil pressure caused him to retire the B.R.M. B.R.M. would dearly have liked Collins in their team for 1956, but like his friend Hawthorn before him, he decided to accept an offer from Enzo Ferrari to join his Formula I team. He also agreed to drive for Aston Martin in their quest for the World's Sports Car Championship.

Had Mercedes-Benz not withdrawn from racing at the end of 1955, it is possible that Collins might have joined Moss and Fangio. Alfred Neubauer was tremendously impressed by Pete, especially after his Targa Florio drive in 1955, when he took over the damaged Mercedes 300SLR from Moss, broke the lap record, and handed over again to Stirling who went on to smash the lap record several times, and clinch the Constructors' Championship for Daimler-Benz. When Collins took over, the car had lost all its water, and had been into the countryside. A deficit of over 12 minutes was turned into a lead of several minutes, although Collins also explored the off-road section. During this really tremendous drive, he hurtled past Castellotti's Ferrari and team-mate Fangio's Mercedes.

Merely driving in the same team as Juan Manuel Fangio in 1956 completely changed Peter Collins's outlook. From having a kind of playboy attitude to the sport, he soon became a dedicated Grand Prix driver. Fortunately his nature remained the same, and he retained the bubbling sense of humour that made him so popular with everyone. Following Fangio, he studied his methods, and with every practice and race lap learned that much more of the art of motor racing.

Collins soon justified Enzo Ferrari's choice, by winning the Belgian G.P. at Spa-Francorchamps, and the French G.P. at Rheims. The newcomer had, in his first season of Formula I, become a leading contender for the Championship of the World. At Monza, the Italian Grand Prix (G.P. d'Europe) was to decide the destination of the title.

H.W.M. introduction to the Grands Prix (French G.P., 1952)

162

A 'really tremendous drive' (Targa Florio, 1955)

Fangio, attempting to win the crown for the fifth time, had abandoned on the nineteenth lap when his steering went haywire. Musso was signalled to come in and hand over to the Argentinian, but either ignored, or chose not to see, the frantic signals. The Italian eventually did stop, but stubbornly refused to surrender the wheel, so Fangio shrugged, and team manager Sculatti gave Musso the O.K. to continue.

Moss was well in the lead with his Maserati, and the only challenge to him could come from the Ferraris of Collins and Musso. Then in came Collins for a quick tyre-check and suddenly realized that with Moss having gained a vital point for fastest lap, Fangio's championship hopes had gone. Sculatti gave a sort of half-hearted gesture, but even before that, Pete was out of his car, and had given Fangio the 'climb in' sign. It is now a matter of history that Juan Manuel drove a cool and calculated race to achieve second place, and, with the points shared with Collins, took the title. There was some poetic justice in that Musso's steering broke and he nearly demolished the pit counter. Moss ran out of fuel, but by a most odd coincidence, as the Maserati was coming to a halt, it was given a push by Piotti (Maserati), who claimed that he couldn't stop as he had run out of brakes. Anyway the nudge was sufficient to roll Moss' car into the pits for a rapid refill. In the closing stages, Moss was slowed down because of tyre wear, and was nearly caught by Fangio. Actually, Collins might have won the Championship himself, but his sportsmanship in handing over to Fangio will be for ever remembered in the annals of Grand Prix racing.

Hawthorn's rather abortive season with B.R.M. and Vanwall had made him all the more eager to rejoin Ferrari. To Pete's delight, Mike was signed on and the two British drivers were also committed to sports-car racing in a team which comprised Musso, Castellotti, de Portago, Phil Hill and Gendebien. However, it was a poor year for the Prancing Horse in Grands Prix for the team did not score a single victory in World Championship events (although Pete did win non-championship races in Syracuse and Naples). With Phil Hill he was second with the 4·1-litre sports-racer at Nürburgring and in Sweden, and was one of the many drivers who swopped Ferraris in the heat-wave of the Argentina 1000-km. race, in which he eventually shared a third place. He also won the extraordinary Caracas race, when the entire Maserati team crashed and wrecked the cars (this indirectly led the Modena concern almost to bankruptcy and to their abandoning motor racing).

Castellotti having lost his life testing a prototype at Modena, the Ferrari Grand Prix team for 1958 comprised Hawthorn, Collins, Musso and Taffy von Trips. It is a sad thought that not one of them is alive today, nor is Fon de Portago, who was reserve G.P. driver and a sports car 'regular'. The Argentinian race was expected to be a complete walk-over for Ferrari's new 2·5-litre cars, but Stirling Moss produced a major sensation when he won with Rob Walker's sadly under-rated 2·2-litre Cooper-Climax. Collins went out with transmission trouble a few minutes after the start.

Ferrari again failed at Monaco, Trintignant winning with the Walker Cooper and Collins having to be content with third place behind his team-mate Musso. Scuderia Ferrari had another bad day at Zandvoort, the red cars all being doubled by Moss's Vanwall, while Pete Collins's gearbox seized. In the Belgian Grand Prix at Spa-Francorchamps, a lengthy delay on the starting line caused Collins's engine to overheat, and this led to his early retirement. Musso completely wrecked his car

Giro di Sicilia, 1956

Last G.P. victory, Silverstone, 1958

at Stavelot, and Hawthorn, missing his friend Collins, immediately thought that Pete's car was involved. This upset him so much, that he began to lose ground to the leader, Brooks (Vanwall). Later, to his immense relief, he spotted both Musso and Collins in the pits, and immediately his driving was transformed. With Pete out on the front apron giving him signals, Mike started to pile on the pressure. Despite a new record lap of 3 minutes 59·3 seconds, it seemed to be a hopeless task, for Tony Brooks had a very big lead.

That last lap will go down in history. Collins held out his private sign to Hawthorn—a chalked drawing of a beer mug. The race still seemed to be a certainty for Brooks. However, coming down to La Source hairpin, his gearbox seized, and the Vanwall began to crawl— fortunately downhill—towards the finishing line. Then Hawthorn stormed into view, almost broadsided, and then went flat out after the slowing Vanwall. A few yards after the hairpin, the Ferrari engine literally exploded, and Mike also coasted over the line. Nevertheless he had set up another lap record with 3 minutes 58·3 seconds. The drama was not yet over, for Lewis-Evans (Vanwall) had his front suspension collapse as he took the flag.

With three victories by British cars in a row, the drivers worked with the Ferrari technicians to try and overcome road-holding problems. They also tried to persuade Enzo to change over to R5 Dunlops, but the Commendatore, always faithful to his commitments, refused to abandon Engleberts. Anyway the Belgian concern came up with a revised tyre, which they said ought to do the trick.

Although Hawthorn retrieved Ferrari fortunes by winning the French G.P. at Rheims, the unfortunate Peter Collins ran out of fuel on the last lap and had to push his car from Thillois for a well-earned fifth place. This was, however, a tragic day for Ferrari for Musso lost his life after crashing at the notorious right-hander just past the pits.

At Silverstone, it was Peter Collins's day for he achieved a lifelong ambition, in winning the British Grand Prix. Earlier, in May, he had won the B.R.D.C. *Daily Express* International Trophy in a car which steered like a tractor and possessed dreadful road-holding. The G.P. was rather a remarkable race in its way, for Sculati had given Collins the job of 'Vanwall-Buster', to help Hawthorn who was running neck-and-neck for the Championship.

Collins was in tremendous form and rocketed into the lead, chased by Moss. Peter set such a furious pace, that by twenty laps he had raised the race average to over 102 m.p.h. When Moss's engine failed, Collins had a huge lead over Hawthorn, and Sculati could not afford to take the risk of slowing him down. However, with Mike's second place and a point for fastest lap, he now led Moss by 7 points in the Championship table. Collins had certainly proved himself to be the perfect team-mate.

No one was to realize that the German Grand Prix at Nürburgring would be Peter Collins's last race. Just after the tenth lap, when Tony Brooks had taken the lead from Collins and with Hawthorn close behind him, Pete attempted to overtake the Vanwall at Pflanzgarten. This is a climbing right-hander, and, according to Hawthorn, Pete decided to hold back and try again later. To Mike's horror, the Ferrari suddenly slewed sideways, and crashed into the bank. There appeared to be no valid reason why this should happen, for up until the time of the crash. Collins was confident and in complete charge of the situation.

Hawthorn seemed to sense that a tragedy had occurred, and it may not have been a coincidence that he over-revved his engine and abandoned. His fears were justified. Despite efficient organization in rushing the popular British driver to hospital by helicopter, Peter Collins succumbed to his injuries.

One of the saddest aspects of following the Grand Prix Circus, is that, from time to time, accidents do happen, and one loses yet another friend. The memory of that Gay Cavalier Pete Collins will remain with all of us, serving to remind us that whilst accidents are not inevitable, they can happen to the most skilful, and indeed no one can deny that 'Motor Racing is Dangerous'.

Peter Collins was held in high esteem by everyone with whom he came in contact. Mechanics, especially, would do anything for him. He was always ready to help them, but never interfered in the preparation of cars. Although he did possess a certain amount of technical knowledge, he would never suggest anything that would involve the mechanics in needless endeavour. He always maintained that he was hired to drive the cars, not to design them.

Ferrari has lost many drivers during the past several years, but whenever Peter Collins's name is mentioned, the Commendatore will reminisce: 'That was a really great one.'

The principal race successes of **PETER COLLINS**

1952	1st:	Goodwood Nine Hours
1953	1st:	Tourist Trophy.
	2nd:	Goodwood Nine Hours.
	3rd:	Eifelrennen.
1954	1st:	Snetterton f.l. Race; Whitsun Trophy, Goodwood; Woodcote Cup; Silverstone Sports Car Race.
	2nd:	Crystal Palace Trophy; Goodwood Trophy.
	3rd:	Buenos Aires 1000 km.
1955	1st:	Targa Florio; Aintree f.l. Race; Chichester Cup; International Trophy, Silverstone.
	2nd:	Le Mans 24-hour Race.
	3rd:	Goodwood Nine Hours; *Daily Herald* International Trophy, Oulton Park.
1956	1st:	Belgian G.P.; French G.P.; Tour of Sicily; Supercortemaggiore G.P.
	2nd:	British G.P.; Italian G.P.; Monaco G.P.; Mille Miglia; Swedish G.P.
	3rd:	Syracuse G.P.
1957	1st:	Naples G.P.; Syracuse G.P.; Venezuelan G.P.
	2nd:	Nürburgring 1000 km; Swedish G.P.
	3rd:	French G.P.; Buenos Aires 1000 km.
1958	1st:	British G.P.; Buenos Aires 1000 km; Sebring 12 hours; International Trophy, Silverstone.
	2nd:	Rheims Coupe de Vitesse; Nürburgring 1000 km; Sussex Trophy, Goodwood.
	3rd:	Monaco G.P.

Nürburgring, German G.P., 1961.

STIRLING MOSS

by DENIS JENKINSON

ANYONE who was lucky enough to have seen Stirling Moss in his first competitive season must have realized that they were seeing a rather special driver in action. Although he was only 17 years old, and not possessed of any racing experience, or for that matter any particularly outstanding technique, it was immediately apparent that here was a driver with a difference. Just how great that difference was going to become nobody could have known, least of all Moss himself. The year was 1948 and he was taking part in speed hill-climbs with a 500-c.c. Cooper-JAP; I remember it well, for at the time my full-time job was in motor cycle racing and I had been watching 500-c.c. car events now and then, feeling that the drivers of the time were not exploiting the characteristics of the single-cylinder motor cycle engine and positive-stop gearchange of the motor cycle gearbox to the fullest extent. On one visit back to England that summer some friends said I should see the new wonder-boy Stirling Moss, a woolly-headed lad who was assisted by his mother and father and carried his racing car about in a horse-box. He was putting up some outstanding performances in speed trials and my first experience of Moss was to hear him before I actually saw him. It was at a speed trial where part of the course came along one side of a hedge, round a hairpin bend and up the other side, and I was standing on the return side. The sound of a Cooper 500 arriving under heavy braking with the gearbox being used like a motor cycle to assist slowing down, made me realize that here was a driver who was well out of the rut of the ordinary 500-c.c. men. The car swept round the hairpin and was gone, the whole manœuvre being done with the engine running at its peak r.p.m., even to the extent of slipping the motor cycle clutch on the apex of the hairpin. He could not have done better had he been on a motor cycle.

I did not need to ask who it was. But I had no idea that many years later I should get to know Stirling Moss so well that I would find how impossible he could be and why, nor that I should motor some 12,000 very high-speed miles with him, and be in the best position to appreciate the uncanny skill that he was to develop—and I doubt whether he realized to what heights he was going to soar. Of one thing I am certain—that he knew he was going to become a professional racing driver and was going to win many races.

In those early days the old pre-war Grand Prix drivers were beginning to fade away and a new era of drivers was appearing, but due to rather misguided patriotism Moss was a long while joining the *élite* of the Grand Prix field.

While 500-c.c. racing taught him a lot about track craft and wheel-to-wheel fighting it did not teach him the finer points of high-speed driving for the little cars were just not fast enough to get into the realms where driving becomes an art, nor had they sufficient power to allow the driver to indulge in any of the higher forms of cornering. However,

Silverstone, 1948

they did allow a driver to develop quick reflexes and a sense of balance, and these two things Moss had in abundance right from the start.

Due to his patriotism and thus his desire to race British cars it was not until 1954 that Moss was able to meet the best Grand Prix drivers on equal terms. Up to that time he raced all manner of cars in all manner of events but while he had many successes and was undoubtedly the best British driver he was inevitably at a disadvantage when racing against the top Continental drivers who ruled the Grands Prix in those days. Even so, many of his brilliant characteristics were developing fast; among these were the ability to go fast at all times, whether practising or racing or merely testing, to put up a fight against overwhelming odds, to set such a cracking pace that not only the opposition fell by the wayside, but sometimes his own car gave out under the strain, and a sense of urgency and thoroughness that was outstanding, especially in a British driver. In those formative years he drove Jaguar, B.R.M., Cooper, H.W.M., Kieft and many others, but he also turned down an offer from Enzo Ferrari because the Italian's demands were too binding. This was an unfortunate decision because Ferrari said he could provide the means to make Stirling Moss a World Champion before Alberto Ascari, and Ascari was Champion in 1952 and 1953!

In 1954 Moss swallowed his nationalistic pride and drove an Italian Maserati, immediately showing a natural brilliance with a real Grand Prix car that was unquestionable. Until I could see Moss on equal terms with such drivers as Fangio, Farina, Ascari, Villoresi and Taruffi I was not prepared to assess his true worth as a racing driver, but in 1954 I accepted the fact that in Stirling Moss Britain had a driver the equal of any, who was fast developing his own techniques of driving that were not only of the highest standard but were bringing high-speed driving into the realms of an art. When it became known that the Mercedes-Benz team were re-entering racing, Stirling Moss's manager Ken Gregory went to see Herr Alfred Neubauer, the team chief, to offer them the services of his driver, at a price. Neubauer told him that the price was unimportant, what they were not convinced about was the ability of Moss as a Grand Prix driver.

He had had plenty of experience with 500-c.c. cars, sports cars and low-powered British racing cars, but none with competitive Grand Prix cars. Neubauer suggested that Moss bought a Maserati and let people see that he was a Grand Prix driver, and this he did. I watched his initial private trial runs on the latest 250F Maserati early in 1954, by mid-season the Maserati factory had asked him to join their team, by the end of the season he was right at the top. So well did he demonstrate his skill that Neubauer signed him up for the 1955 season as number two driver to the great J. M. Fangio.

During 1955 Moss really developed as a Grand Prix driver, for he spent the whole season in the wheel tracks of the acknowledged master, learning more in that season than all the others put together. From there he went on to even greater things first leading the Vanwall team to victory after victory until they set the seal on Britain's supremacy in Grand Prix racing and following this by driving Rob Walker's Cooper-Climax and Lotus-Climax cars to many more victories, playing a substantial role in giving Great Britain a supremacy in Grand Prix racing undreamed of when he first started in motoring competitions.

In 1955 Moss invited me to ride with him in the Mille Miglia and through this I got to know him extremely well, both as a driver and a

(left) Single-seater apprenticeship. Cooper,
Silverstone, 1949 . . .

Single-seater maturity.
Mercedes-Benz, Aintree, 1955 . . .

(left) . . . H.W.M., Bremgarten, 1951 . . .

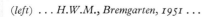

. . . Vanwall, Silverstone, 1958 . . .

(left) . . . Maserati, Monza, 1954

. . . Cooper, Zandvoort, 1959

person. As a driver he was faultless, as a person he could be tiresome. No matter what the car was he instilled a fantastic feeling of confidence in me, and even though we had numerous racing accidents together, none were serious and I never lost my confidence in his ability to handle a car under any conditions. Most racing drivers I have ridden with have an ability along the same lines as my own, but with a far higher degree of skill and courage than I possess, but Moss seemed to take me into a different world, doing things with a car that I could not foresee, deliberately provoking slides at times when I would imagine he would not want it to slide; forcing the car to do what he wanted it to do, rather than working at high pressure to keep abreast of what the car wanted to do. I have always maintained that the artistry of Moss was such that he could provoke a car into developing the handling characteristics he thought best for the conditions, rather than waiting to see what the natural tendencies of the car were and acting accordingly. In this way he always seemed to be a fraction ahead of the car all the time, whereas most drivers are a fraction behind their car most of the time, and only occasionally alongside it.

His faculties of eyesight, judgement, anticipation and reflexes were all of an outstandingly high order and worked in a rare unison. These natural attributes that made him a super-man and in consequence sometimes very difficult to live with when not racing.

He could never relax, take unnecessary time over a meal, read a book or listen to a symphony—he was always on the go, from the moment he got up to the moment he went to bed. His one good attribute, from my point of view, was an unwillingness to get up early in the morning! On this we agreed, but on many other things we agreed to differ, he would run where I would walk, he would do a high-speed sight-seeing tour of shop windows while I would lie down and rest after a long day's motoring. He would turn a shoe shop inside out and not buy a thing, whereas I would buy the first likely-looking pair of shoes. He would insist on certain food and drink in the most unlikely little restaurants in Italy, and complain when he couldn't get them, whereas I would accept what was offered. From leaving school at a relatively early age he had lived a completely artificial life of travel, hotels, publicity, glamour and racing; after a week or ten days of this non-stop high pressure I would have to leave him and go away to regain my sense of proportion, and sit in the sun and read a book, or just sit and cogitate— something that Moss could not do and would not let his companions do. Not because of a mean streak in him but because he was always active and up to something and it involved whoever was with him.

Skin diving, water skiing or speed boat riding, and so on, all these interludes were holidays between motor races. He would go dancing until 4 a.m.—all on nothing stronger than Coca-Cola—and whereas most people would unwind as the hours wore on, passing the last hour in lazy conversation over a coffee or a brandy, Moss would suddenly reach his limit and stop instantly and within five minutes would be in bed and asleep, gathering energy for another whirlwind day.

While being very tiresome to live with this dynamic force was a terrific morale booster for a racing team, for from the moment he arrived for testing or practice the whole air became electrified and he had people running in all directions, timekeepers, mechanics, engineers, they all worked with an urgency that was doubled by the presence of Stirling Moss. His driving at all times was the same, I don't think he

British Sports cars. Jaguar, Silverstone, 1951 . . .

. . . Aston Martin, Oulton Park, 1958

ever had an off-day and did not know the meaning of defeat or the impossible. The more impossible a situation appeared the harder he would try and some of his finest races were not those he won, but those he lost.

In races where mechanical trouble had delayed him and put him back down the field he would then drive with a brilliance that was unsurpassable, to forge his way back to second or third place, with lap record after lap record, knowing he could not catch the leader, but nevertheless having a darned good try. He probably shone more brightly on such occasions than when he won races by leading from start to finish, for then he left the other drivers behind him looking like amateurs. His driving at all times was absolutely correct and that of a gentleman, he never indulged in dubious manœuvres or dirty play. He didn't have to, he could beat most people without trying, although he admits that Fangio was always his master in Grand Prix racing.

In many ways Moss was his own worst rival, for he would make unnecessary experiments with his cars when he could beat all the opposition with a perfectly standard vehicle. But he always maintained that you could never tell when new opposition was going to appear and only by continually experimenting with new ideas could you be prepared for any eventuality. Unfortunately, however, many of these experiments let him down when victory would have been easy.

He never won the Drivers' World Championship for during his rising years he was always behind Fangio. When that great Argentinian driver retired Moss was undisputed number one in Grand Prix racing but lost the Championship due to mechanical misfortunes and bad mechanical judgement on his own part, choosing the wrong car or wrong component. This was because he was always seeking perfection and would not accept that he was perfection as a driver, which should have been sufficient. He tried to assist in design and preparation and the results were not as good as his driving.

His racing career came to an untimely end at Goodwood in 1962 when he crashed badly and lost the superbly co-ordinated faculties of eyesight and judgement that had put him way out ahead of normal people. This final crash transformed these outstanding features into merely average ones, so that he decided wisely to retire from racing. It was a very hard decision to make but with only average eyesight, judgement, anticipation and reflexes he could never retain the high standards he knew, and to be a mediocre racing driver was untenable.

In his long racing career Moss had crashed many times, sometimes having lucky escapes, sometimes hurting himself, but always returning to his former heights. It must have been more than a year before I could convince myself that he had driven his last race and had had his last crash. I always felt that this super-man could not be beaten, but finally I had to realize that Stirling Moss was really just another human being, just as frail and fragile as any other and just as vulnerable. The outstanding faculties that nature had given him had been taken away and he was now an ordinary mortal, destined to do no more great things at the wheel of a racing car. At the height of his career, around 1955–7, a friend called him a 'Golden Boy'. To me he will always be *the* Golden Boy of motor racing.

Two of his three most outstanding drives:
(above) Mille Miglia, 1955 (below) German G.P., 1961

The principal racing successes of **STIRLING MOSS**

1948   1st: Goodwood F.3 race.

1949   1st: Madgwick Cup, Goodwood; Silverstone F.3 Race; Zandvoort F.3 Race.

   3rd: Circuit of Garda.

1950   1st: Tourist Trophy; Prix de Monte Carlo; Two Brands Hatch F.3 Races; Nürburgring F.3 Race.

   2nd: Mettet F.2 Race; Perigeux F.2 Race; Silverstone F.3 Race.

   3rd: Coupe des Petites Cylindrées, Rheims; Bari G.P.

1951   1st: Tourist Trophy; Empire Trophy; Wakefield Trophy; Lavant Trophy, Goodwood; Madgwick Cup, Goodwood; Brands Hatch F.3 Race; Goodwood F.3 Race; Silverstone F.3 Race; Zandvoort F.3 Race.

   2nd: Aix le Bains F.2 Race; Winfield F.2 Race.

   3rd: Dutch G.P.; Marseilles G.P.; Autodrome G.P., Monza.

1952   1st: Rheims Sports Car Race; Boreham Sports Car Race; Turnberry Sports Car Race; Brands Hatch F.3 Race; Castle Combe F.3 Race; Three Goodwood F.3 Races; Silverstone F.3 Race.

   2nd: Eifelrennen; Charterhall F.3 Race.

   3rd: *Daily Mail* Trophy (F.2) Boreham.

1953   1st: Rheims 12-hour Race; London Trophy, Crystal Palace; Charterhall F.3 Race; Silverstone F.3 Race; Silverstone Touring Car Race.

   2nd: Le Mans 24-Hour Race; Lisbon G.P.; Madgwick Cup, Goodwood; Ulster Trophy, Heat 1.

   3rd: Sables d'Olonne G.P.

1954   1st: Sebring 12 hours; Aintree 200; Aintree f.l. Race; *Daily Telegraph* Trophy, Aintree; Goodwood Trophy; Oulton Park Gold Cup; Oulton Park f.l. Race.

   2nd: Caen G.P.

   3rd: Belgian G.P.; Woodcote Cup.

1955   1st: British G.P.; Tourist Trophy; Targa Florio; Mille Miglia; Governors Cup, Lisbon; Oulton Park Gold Cup.

   2nd: Belgian G.P.; Dutch G.P.; Eifelrennen; Swedish G.P.; Buenos Aires G.P.

   3rd: Redex Trophy, Snetterton; Chichester Cup, Goodwood.

1956   1st: Italian G.P.; Monaco G.P.; Bari G.P.; Buenos Aires 1000 km; Nassau Trophy; Venezuelan G.P.; Australian G.P.; Australian T.T.; New Zealand G.P.; Empire Trophy; London Trophy; Norbury Trophy, Crystal Palace; Glover Trophy; Aintree 200; Silver-

stone Sports Car Race; *Daily Herald* International Trophy, Oulton Park; International Trophy, Silverstone.

   2nd: German G.P.; Rouen G.P.; Nürburgring Sports Car Race; Supercortemaggiore G.P.; Anerley Trophy.

   3rd: Belgian G.P.; Le Mans 24-hour Race; Nürburgring 1000 km.

1957   1st: British G.P.; Italian G.P.; Pescara G.P.; Swedish G.P.; Nassau Trophy.

   2nd: Buenos Aires 1000 km; Sebring 12 hours.

   3rd: Syracuse G.P.

1958   1st: Argentine G.P.; Dutch G.P.; Portuguese G.P.; Moroccan G.P.; Caen G.P.; Coupe de Vitesse, Rheims; Nürburgring 1000 km; Sussex Trophy Goodwood; Aintree 200; Circuit of Villa Real; Kannonskloppet; Silverstone Sports Car Race; Kentish 100; Cuban G.P.; Melbourne G.P.; Tourist Trophy; Empire Trophy .

   2nd: French G.P.; Roskilde Sports Car Race.

   3rd: Buenos Aires 1000 km.

1959   1st: Italian G.P.; Portuguese G.P.; Circuit d'Auvergne; Roskilde Sports Car Race; Rouen G.P.; Rouen Sports Car Race; Oulton Park Gold Cup; Nürburgring 1000 km; Syracuse G.P.; Kannonskloppet; Governors Trophy, Nassau; Watkins Glen f.l. Race; New Zealand G.P.; Tourist Trophy; Glover Trophy.

   2nd: British G.P.

1960   1st: Monaco G.P.; Nürburgring 1000 km; Kannonskloppet; Redex Trophy, Brands Hatch; Cape G.P.; Aintree 200; Cuban G.P.; Pacific G.P.; Watkins Glen f.l. Race; Tourist Trophy; Fordwater Trophy, Goodwood; Oulton Park Gold Cup.

   2nd: Brussels G.P.; Lavant Trophy; South African G.P.; Nassau T.T.; Sebring 1-litre G.T. Race; Glover Trophy.

   3rd: Argentine G.P.

1961   1st: German G.P.; Monaco G.P.; International Trophy, Silverstone; Tourist Trophy; Silverstone Sports Car Race; Copenhagen G.P.; Oulton Park Gold Cup; Sussex Trophy, Goodwood; Lavant Trophy; Aintree Sports Car Race; Silver City Trophy, Brands Hatch; Kannonskloppet; Empire Trophy; Pacific G.P.; Warwick Farm 100; Nassau T.T.; Players 200; Lady Wigram Trophy.

   2nd: South African G.P.; Natal G.P.

   3rd: Canadian G.P.

1962   1st: Warwick Farm 100; New Zealand G.P.; Lady Wigram Trophy.

   2nd: Hudson Trophy, Levin; Invercargill Trophy.

   3rd: Sebring 1-litre G.T. Race.

THE CONTRIBUTORS

L. SCOTT BAILEY — Editor and publisher of 'Automobile Quarterly' since 1962 (when he launched this hard-cover journal); earlier editor of the Antique Automobile Club journal 'Antique Automobile'. Joint author—with his wife—of *Buy an Antique Automobile*.

AL BLOEMKER — Energetic public relations director of the Indianapolis Motor Speedway. Author of two books on the '500', *The Exciting 500* and *500 Miles To Go*.

WILLIAM BODDY — Motoring historian and journalist, editor of 'Motor Sport' since 1945. Author of several books on motoring and motor racing, including *The History of the Brooklands Motor Course, Montlhéry, 1924–60* and *The Sports Car Pocket Book*.

W. F. BRADLEY — Pioneer 'Continental Correspondent', covered many early races for 'The Motor' and 'The Autocar'. Author of several books, including a history of the Targa Florio.

GIANNI CANCELLIERI — Sports Editor of the Italian journal 'Autosprint'.

S. C. H. DAVIS — Motoring journalist, sometime racing driver. Launched 'Automobile Engineer', 1912, member of the staff of 'The Autocar', 1919–50. Won two B.R.D.C. Gold Stars, two A.C.O. Gold Medals (and, with Benjafield, the legendary 1927 Le Mans 24-Hour Race). Author of numerous books, including *Motor Racing*, *Atalanta* and *The John Cobb Story*.

EDWARD EVES — Sometime member of Rootes Group engineering staff, now a motoring journalist; editor of 'Autocourse' until 1959 and present Midlands Editor of 'Autocar'.

RICHARD VON FRANKENBERG — Motoring writer and sometime racing driver, notably with Porsches in the fifties. Author of motor racing histories in the German language.

JOHN EASON GIBSON — Secretary of the British Racing Drivers' Club, journalist (Motoring Editor of 'Country Life'), sometime racing driver and team manager. Author of *Motor Racing*, 1946–48.

GREGOR GRANT — Motoring journalist, sometime Assistant Editor of 'The Light Car' and since 1950, when he founded the journal, Managing Editor of 'Autosport'. Author of several books, including *500-c.c. Racing*, *Formula 2 Racing* and *World Championship*.

DAVID HODGES — Member of the Publisher's editorial staff, contributor to motoring journals and author of the first two books in the 'Classic Motor Races' Series, *The Le Mans 24-Hour Race* and *The Monaco Grand Prix*.

JACQUES ICKX — Motoring historian and journalist. Author of the Guild of Motoring Writers Award-winning *Ainsi Naquit l'Automobile*.

Motoring writer, Continental Correspondent of 'Motor Sport'. Author of the annual *'Motor Sport' Racing Car Reviews* (1947–56), *The Racing Driver*, *A Story of Formula I* and *The Racing Car Pocket Book*.

DENIS JENKINSON

Journalist and book editor, car enthusiast and Managing Editor of 'Automobile Quarterly'.

MERVIN KAUFMAN

Authority on motor racing in South America and contributor to British motoring journals. Author of a biography of Juan Manuel Fangio.

FEDERICO KIRBUS

'Johnny Lurani', Dott. Ing. Count Giovanni Lurani Cernuschi. Motoring writer and sometime racing driver, 'Father of Formula Junior'. Author of a biography of Nuvolari.

GIOVANNI LURANI

Authority on Italian motoring history and correspondent in that country of 'Autosport'.

GIANNI MARIN

Motoring journalist and historian, sometime Associate Editor of 'Autosport' and Editor of 'Motoring News'; since 1963 a member of the staff of 'Motor'. Author of numerous books, including *The British Competition Car*, *Sir Henry Segrave*, *World Sports Car Championship* and, most recently, *The German Grand Prix* in the 'Classic Motor Races' Series.

CYRIL POSTHUMUS

American-in-Europe motoring journalist, contributor to many American and European journals.

JERRY SLONIGER

Motoring journalist, sometime member of the staff of E.R.A. Ltd. Joined 'Motor' in 1953, Sports Editor since 1959.

PHILIP TURNER

Motoring writer, Sports Editor of 'The Motor', 1934–58. Author of numerous books on motoring and motor sport, including *Brooklands to Goodwood—A History of the B.A.R.C.* and *Automobile Racing*.

RODNEY WALKERLEY

ILLUSTRATIONS

The publishers are grateful to those organizations and individuals who have supplied the photographs reproduced in this book. In particular to the editor of *Motor*, for most of the photographs were taken for that journal, and to B.M.W. (lower photograph, page 93); Mr. W. F. Bradley (pages 9, 49, 82); Daimler-Benz A.G. (pages 2, 4, 5, 14, 16, 65, (*top*), 69 (*top*), 125); Signor Gianni Cancellieri (pages 38, 43 (*top*), 44); S.A. Fiat (pages 11 (*top*), 21, 30, 39); Mr. John Eason Gibson (pages 52, 54 (*bottom*), 110, 113 (*centre*)); The Indianapolis Motor Speedway (pages 134, 138, 139); Louis Klemantaski Ltd. (page 164); The Long Island Automotive Museum (page 18); Automobiles Peugeot S.A. (pages 22, 24); Mr. Cyril Posthumus (pages 12, 19, 20, 65 (*bottom*), 89, 133); Shell-Mex and B.P. Ltd. (page 32).